FOREWORD BY JEN WILKIN

# enough
# about me

FIND LASTING JOY
IN THE AGE OF SELF

jen oshman

"Lord knows that we have more than enough books about ourselves and never enough books about the God that created us. It isn't until we see him that we can then make sense of ourselves. I believe Jen Oshman's book accomplishes that by widening our vision and helping us fall in love with seeing God again."

**Jackie Hill Perry,** poet; author; hip-hop artist

"Countless voices are telling women, 'Believe in yourself . . . reach your potential . . . find your purpose . . . fulfill your destiny.' But *Enough about Me* has a very different message, a message that is not only countercultural but also runs counter to today's Christian culture: your life is not ultimately or most profoundly about you, but about the one who has made you his own. This is the kind of good news women really need."

**Nancy Guthrie,** Bible teacher; author, *Even Better than Eden: Nine Ways the Bible's Story Changes Everything about Your Story*

"The siren call of self promises much but provides little. While the world tells us to want more, do more, and be more, Jen Oshman turns our eyes from ourselves and helps us to find our lives in Jesus, the giver of every good and perfect gift. Written with warmth and wisdom, *Enough about Me* is an encouragement to something better, something richer, and something true."

**Melissa B. Kruger,** Director of Women's Content, The Gospel Coalition; author, *In All Things* and *Growing Together*

"Jen Oshman deftly walks through a variety of challenges to following Jesus in the modern world. Each time she helpfully exposes the shortcomings of living for the self, while also pointing to the joy of living for and in Christ. I will give a copy to each of my daughters and pray they absorb Oshman's godly instruction."

**Jonathan K. Dodson,** Founding Pastor, City Life Church, Austin, Texas; Founder, Gospel-Centered Discipleship; author, *The Unbelievable Gospel*; *Here in Spirit*; and *Our Good Crisis*

"For many years now I have benefited from Jen Oshman's writing. I'm delighted that she has broadened her repertoire to include this book. In an age obsessed with self, its message is delightfully countercultural and desperately needed."

**Tim Challies,** blogger, Challies.com

"*Enough about Me* is for those who feel tired, burned out, or like they're not enough. Jen Oshman kindly encourages readers to look away from themselves and to look instead to Jesus, powerfully reminding them that true, lasting joy is found only in him. This book will lift your gaze in a way that will change your life."

**Hunter Beless,** Founder and Host, *Journeywomen* podcast

"This book had me hooked right from the start. I guzzled my coffee as I considered the common struggles of despair and disillusionment Jen Oshman describes. But the real triumph is the way *Enough about Me* turned my eyes to the one who defines my life and gives me joy. This is a must-read for any woman running on empty because her 'fuel of self' has run out. Our empty hearts need to find full dependence on God."

**Emily Jensen,** Cofounder, Risen Motherhood; coauthor, *Risen Motherhood: Gospel Hope for Everyday Moments*

"In a time when our greatest value is self and the lure of this world tricks us into believing we can have it all, I can't think of a more necessary and relevant book for today's women. Jen Oshman masterfully ushers us to where greater joy is found by redirecting our gaze from ourselves to Christ. If you've ever had it all only to be discontent, or you've been discontent with all that you have, this book is for you."

**Shar Walker,** Senior Writer, North American Mission Board

"Every day, disciples of Christ are bombarded with competing information for how they can live their best lives. Whether it's chiseling your arms at the gym, keeping a smokestack of essential oils pumping in your house, or promising to never buy frozen chicken nuggets again—none of these things will sustainably complete you, calm you, or comfort you. The focus on self is crushing us. Jen Oshman reminds readers that the more we focus on *me*, the more out of focus we become. Sisters, there is only one place to look that will secure the good life you truly need: 'Christ who is your life' (Col. 3:4). And in this book, that's who Jen Oshman points you to—Jesus and all his glory. Take up and read. We can never get enough of him."

**J. A. Medders,** author, *Humble Calvinism*; Pastor of Preaching and Theology, Redeemer Church, Tomball, Texas

# Enough about Me

# Enough about Me

Find Lasting Joy
in the Age of Self

Jen Oshman

Foreword by Jen Wilkin

:: **CROSSWAY**®

WHEATON, ILLINOIS

Published in association with the literary agency of Wolgemuth & Associates, Inc.

Cover design: Connie Gabbert, The Spare Button

First printing 2020

Printed in the United States of America

Unless otherwise indicated, Scripture quotations are from the ESV® Bible (The Holy Bible, English Standard Version®), copyright © 2001 by Crossway, a publishing ministry of Good News Publishers. Used by permission. All rights reserved.

Scripture references marked NIV are taken from The Holy Bible, New International Version®, NIV®. Copyright © 1973, 1978, 1984, 2011 by Biblica, Inc.™ Used by permission. All rights reserved worldwide.

All emphases in Scripture quotations have been added by the author.

Trade paperback ISBN: 978-1-4335-6599-1
ePub ISBN: 978-1-4335-6602-8
PDF ISBN: 978-1-4335-6600-4
Mobipocket ISBN: 978-1-4335-6601-1

**Library of Congress Cataloging-in-Publication Data**

Names: Oshman, Jen, 1978– author.
Title: Enough about me : finding lasting joy in the age of self / Jen Oshman.
Description: Wheaton : Crossway, 2020. | Includes bibliographical references and index.
Identifiers: LCCN 2019014551 (print) | LCCN 2019022355 (ebook) | ISBN 9781433565991 (tp)
Subjects: LCSH: Christian women—Religious life. | Identity (Psychology)—Religious
    aspects—Christianity.
Classification: LCC BV4527 .O855 2020 (print) | LCC BV4527 (ebook) | DDC 248.8/43—dc23
LC record available at https://lccn.loc.gov/2019014551
LC ebook record available at https://lccn.loc.gov/2019022355

Crossway is a publishing ministry of Good News Publishers.

BP        30   29   28   27   26   25   24   23   22   21   20
15   14   13   12   11   10   9   8   7   6   5   4   3   2   1

For Mark
No matter the season, the country, or the circumstances, you have always ensured that I flourish. You are a great means of God's grace in my life. I love you.

# Contents

# Foreword

Have you ever found yourself underdressed at a party? It's not the best feeling, especially if that party is a lavish wedding and you are an honored guest. That was me about ten years ago at the wedding of a dear family friend. Two days before the wedding, I received news that my uncle had passed away suddenly. We were able to adjust our plans to make it to both the funeral and the wedding, but a flight delay meant we were faced with the choice of either walking into the wedding ceremony in our simple funeral clothes or missing it altogether.

We decided to go straight to the ceremony, arriving just before the processional began, taking our seats in full view of the entire assembly of well-dressed guests. It makes me sweat just remembering that moment. We hurriedly changed into our wedding attire before the reception, and guess what? Not one person at the reception had even noticed our late entrance or lacking attire at the ceremony. Of course they didn't. As it should be, everyone's attention had been fully fixed on the splendor of the bride and groom. All of my anxiety about inadequate dress had been a waste of energy.

It is common, indeed, epidemic for women to lose sight of their purpose and calling. In a culture that tells us we are the center of everyone's story, every day can feel like another opportunity to be the noticeably underdressed invitee at a party everyone else is attending in full glamour. Comparisons and expectations cause us to self-examine and find ourselves lacking. Anxiety over inadequacy, across days and years.

But the Christian story we are invited into, the best and most beautiful of stories, does not offer us a starring role. It does not place us at the center of the story at all. Which is why it is best and beautiful.

It is the story, in fact, of those invited to a wedding— a story, indeed, of those lately come from a funeral. It is a wedding between a bridegroom (Christ) worthy of all our attention and a bride (the church) worthy of all our effort. It is a story that invites us again and again to remember that we are not the center of attention, but that our lives can be joyfully spent preparing the bride for her husband.

This is the story Jen Oshman intends to tell you. Though your expectations for how life should be, for who you should be, and for how others should see you may daily swirl before your eyes, there is a vision higher than those that can restore to you the joy of your salvation. Oshman calls you to a wedding where the appropriate attire is self-forgetfulness and the liturgy sings the splendor of the Happy Couple. What is more fulfilling than a life spent chasing self-actualization? A life spent giving glory to the God who transcends.

This is the good life. This is the best and most beautiful story.

Welcome to the feast.

Jen Wilkin

# Acknowledgments

Getting this message in readers' hands has been a joy and delight. I am so grateful the Lord allowed me this gift of grace. May he be glorified.

This book would not have been possible without the encouragement of seasoned authors and doors opened to me by those already in the writing world. Thank you, Melissa Kruger, for inviting me to write at The Gospel Coalition, for your friendship, and for your example of championing the word of God as you minister to women. Thank you, Shanna Davis, for reading my words, believing in my message, and making that connection. Thank you, Tim Challies, for reading my blog and sharing it with the world. You elevate so many new writers, and I am humbled to be among them. Thank you, Andrew Wolgemuth, for helping me understand this writing world, still a bit foreign to me. Thank you for your tireless guidance and feedback on every question I have had, whether big or small, and for giving me confidence to move forward. And thank you, Chrissy Wolgemuth, for saying hello almost four years ago and becoming a friend and encourager to me. Thank you, Tara Davis, for sharing your gift of editing with me. Your careful work made this book so strong. Thank you, Jen Wilkin, for your word-centered ministry to women. You have been a mentor from afar. Thank you for leading well and for your generosity in writing the foreword to this book. Finally, thank you, Dave DeWit, for taking a risk on a brand-new author. You have been a wise and kind shepherd to me at every step.

Thank you to our prayer and financial supporters who have poured into our life of missions and church planting for two decades. Your investment in the kingdom through our work with Cadence International, Pioneers International, and Redemption Parker has been more than humbling to my family. We truly could not be in ministry if it weren't for your commitment to the gospel and to the Oshmans. Thank you for enabling me to write this book.

I am forever grateful for friends who have persisted over the years and over the miles. Thank you, Jen Rathmell and Kristie Coia, for being constant sources of strength, grace, and truth. And to all the women from our years at the Harbor in Okinawa and Betanie in Czechia, you have played a role in growing me and shaping the message of this book. I miss you.

Thank you to my nearby friends, who persevered through conversations and prayer times when I wondered if I should even give this a try. Thank you, Sue Toussaint, Alivia Russo, and Allie Slocum, for memorizing Colossians with me—surely those were the seeds of this book. Thank you, ladies of Redemption Parker, for letting me bounce ideas off of you, and for your enthusiasm for this message. Thank you for studying the Bible with me, praying with me and for me, and for your encouragement in these pages. Thank you,

Joe and Whitney Finke, for reading my first chapters and sharing your photography and writing skills. Thank you to the women in my Gospel Community for being tireless cheerleaders. Thank you, Sandie Dugas, for your partnership in the gospel, abiding friendship, and for being equal parts godly and hilarious.

To my "freditors," thank you for your devotion and care. Thank you, Kim Forney, for your tireless support and pressing me where my words were weak—you make me a better writer. Thank you, Carrie Abraham, for more than I can say. Not only did you read every single word of my manuscript with scrutiny and kindness, you and Chris have laid down your lives for us time and time again.

Thank you, Mom, for taking me to church three decades ago. You enabled me to hear the gospel and receive the life-changing grace of Jesus. Thanks, too, for instilling in me a love of reading and writing from an early age. Thank you, Rebekah, Zoe, Abby Grace, and Hannah, for being life-giving daughters. I genuinely love being your mom. Thank you for allowing me the space and time to write this book and for being as excited as I am about it. Thank you, Mark, for loving me like Christ loves the church. You've invested more in me than any other human—the words in this book come from you as much as they do me. I could not have envisioned or asked for a better colaborer for life across three continents, with four daughters, and over two decades of marriage so far.

And to my God in heaven, apart from you I can do nothing. Thank you for rescuing and redeeming me.

# Introduction

I sat, exhausted, on my dorm room floor, my eyes hot, my head throbbing. My tear ducts were dry, and my mind was limping along wondering how I ended up like this. The sadness enveloping me was foreign. I had always been happy and successful—things usually went well for me. And now I couldn't even identify what was pushing the battering ram into my middle.

I was eighteen and enjoying my quintessential first year of college. My days were filled with green quads, captivating classes, and social gatherings. What was there to cry about?

And yet day after day, for weeks, I was stricken with a grief that seemed, at first, to have no source. I was just mournful.

Now I look back on those days with gratitude. I can see from here that they were a gift of grace, a tool in God's hands to draw me to himself. But at the time I felt as if I were under water, unable to catch my breath, disoriented from swimming so hard and making no progress.

Maybe you can relate. Perhaps you too have charted a course and worked hard, only to arrive at a goal that didn't deliver what you thought it would.

While college was the first time I encountered such disillusionment, it wouldn't be the last. As a young wife, I quickly learned that marriage wasn't exactly what I had anticipated. My entrance into professional life as a young adult was rife with disappointment. Even my life in Christian ministry has had its share of valleys. My midlife too—a season that's supposed to be the pinnacle, the climax, the destination—doesn't match the movies or the imaginings I had as a young girl.

How many times have you arrived at your desired destinations only to find that they did not deliver on their promises? We're left tired. Cynical. Disappointed in what life has produced for us.

In the two decades I've been in women's ministry, I've encountered this story time and time again. My friend Leila always wanted a big family. Now that she's the mom of five little ones, she's frustrated, resentful that her husband doesn't help around the home, and drowning in behavioral issues with several of her young boys. A single friend, Andrea, has climbed the corporate ladder with finesse. While she is making well into six figures and has the business lifestyle she always wanted, she's finding that it falls short of the personal fulfillment she anticipated. And then there's Dana, who seemingly excels at doing it all: work, motherhood, church, kids' sports—the works. But in private she confesses that she feels like a failure at all of them and if she could, she'd run away, if only for a break and a feeble attempt at finding temporary peace.

These stories and confessions aren't unique to the ladies sharing their burdens at Bible study. The wider world notices this phenomenon too. Our present moment bears witness to a growing population of hurting women.

While I don't recommend turning to Oprah for advice, her empire does have its finger on the pulse of today's American women. An Oprah.com article titled "The New Midlife Crises for Women" captures what I'm talking about. The article cites research that "women's happiness has 'declined both absolutely and relative to men' from the early '70s to the mid 2000s. More than one in five women are on antidepressants."[1]

I see this in my own town, where the deteriorating mental health of women is a major public health concern. According to a county human services worker, the suicide rate among women is exceptionally high here in the Denver suburbs. A friend who is an emergency responder shared that his team often answers 911 calls from women who have overdosed on drugs and alcohol—frequently in the middle of the day. A nearby neighbor recently lost her rights to her children after driving them to school while intoxicated.

What is going on? Why are women—from the teen years through midlife and beyond—languishing so? We now have greater access to education, professional opportunities, wealth, and self-determination than ever before. We can seemingly have it all—or at least much more than we had in the past and considerably more than women in other parts of the world. And yet, we're more depressed than ever.

This is not what the giver of life intended.

Back on the floor of my college dorm room, I sat with my dusty Bible that I had brought to college but never opened. Although I believed in God, I didn't know his word. That night, however, I grabbed it like a lifeline, reaching

---

1. Ada Calhoun, "The New Midlife Crisis: Why (and How) It's Hitting Gen X Women," Oprah.com, http://www.oprah.com/sp/new-midlife-crisis.html/, accessed January 2018.

out for something more, something to help me catch my breath, find peace, and heal me.

I arrived at the end of the Gospel of Matthew, where Jesus went to the garden of Gethsemane to pray before he was to endure the cross. What captivated me was that even in his unspeakable grief Jesus prayed to the Father, "Not as I will, but as you will" (Matt. 26:39). In the emotional brutality of Gethsemane I saw a Son sweetly surrendered to his Father, trusting him with immeasurable pain.

My soul longed to trust too. I didn't think then, and I don't think now that my suffering was on par with Jesus's. Even then, as an inexperienced Bible reader, I grasped that my valley of despair was *nothing* compared to the prospect of hanging on a cross and bearing the weight of the world's sins.

But in those pages, I sensed that God was standing ready to heal me. He wanted to provide relief for my sadness. Through his word, it felt like God was saying to me, "Jen, I will heal you. But you've got to give me your *whole* self." In that valley, I knew the Lord was asking me to surrender. I didn't know what that meant or how I might do it. But I longed to be healed.

If you too find yourself sitting on a floor, then this book is for you. Maybe you're on the boardroom floor in your company's office building, or the nursery floor knee-deep in diapers, or the floor of your master bedroom wondering how to repair your marriage. You might be on a floor overseas, or in the heart of a city, or in the middle of nowhere. You may be on a floor you never envisioned, or perhaps you are sitting squarely where you had hoped you would be, but it's not turning out as you thought.

Or maybe you're not on the floor at all right now. If things are going really well for you, rejoice! But we know that in our fallen world, promises are broken and dreams don't always come true. A floor moment is likely coming. On this side of heaven, no one is left unscathed.

Wherever you find yourself, as a woman in this age you are likely battling some disillusionment, disenchantment, or disappointment with what life has brought you. This book will explore both how we got here and how we might get closer to the abundant life that Jesus promised to those who believe (John 10:10).

A brief word of caution before we get started: This book is not meant to address the real challenges of clinical depression. The pages that follow are written with the discouragement in mind that is commonplace among women today. If you suspect that you are experiencing significant mental illness, please seek the wisdom and treatment of a licensed counselor.

In the chapters to come we'll examine the societal norms and practices that have delivered us into our current crisis of unhappiness. We'll step back and ask why the world's wisdom hasn't given us what it promised it would. We'll specifically wrestle with why Christian women are disheartened. Why is it that nearly half of women who attend church say they experience no emotional support there?[2]

After diagnosing how we got here, we'll turn our hearts and minds toward God's word. How did God make us? To what has he called us? How exactly can "the God of hope fill [us] with all joy and peace" (Rom. 15:13)?

---

2. "Five Factors Changing Women's Relationship with Churches," Barna website, June 25, 2015, https://www.barna.com/research/five-factors-changing -womens-relationship-with-churches/.

As we turn these pages together, I hope that we will come to a fuller understanding of the gospel. It is the story of Jesus's life, death, and resurrection. It is the message of salvation. *And it is also our daily hope and source of strength for whatever comes.* God calls us to root ourselves in Christ Jesus the Lord, to be built up in him, and to be established in him (Col. 2:6–7). When we do that, we will find the lasting joy we're looking for.

# 1

# The Siren Call of Self

I am nearing my fortieth birthday. In just a couple weeks my friends and family will gather to celebrate, and I'm looking forward to it. Forty. It's a much-anticipated age.

Did you know that starting in 1970 Jennifer was the most popular name in North America for fourteen years in a row? One news article called it the *Jennifer Juggernaut* because there has never been another name phenomenon like it.[1]

There's an entire generation of us. Just about every third girl in all of my classes from kindergarten through college was named Jennifer, Jen, or Jennie (Or is it spelled Jenny? My grade school worksheets reveal that I never could figure that out.). We are everywhere.

We Jennifers were born when America's favorite films were *Grease*, *Saturday Night Fever*, *Star Wars*, and *The Pink Panther*. Pretty groovy. Bell-bottoms and leisure suits marked

---

1. Jen Gerson, "The Jennifer Epidemic: How the Spiking Popularity of Different Baby Names Cycle Like Genetic Drift," *The National Post*, January 23, 2015, https://nationalpost.com/news/the-jennifer-epidemic-how-the-spiking -popularity-of-different-baby-names-cycle-like-genetic-drift.

the fashion scene. In my birth pictures, my dad is rocking a butterfly collar. My mom's hair is cut in the then-popular pageboy style. With my parents' on-point fashion sense, you know I had to be a Jennifer. Just another sign of the times.

Some of my earliest memories from the 1980s include fashions that I see again now when I go shopping with my daughters: high-waisted jeans and crop tops, shoulder pads, jean jackets, and fanny packs. I'm in favor of the jeans—last year we called them "mom jeans," but my daughters swear that high-waisted jeans are different and immeasurably superior to mom jeans. Whatever the case, this almost-forty mom is happy to say sayonara to low-rise denim. But do we have to be so quick to welcome back fanny packs and shoulder pads?

If you can identify any of these popular fashion items, then you might be part of Generation X, of which I am just barely a member—the cutoff is 1981. The millennials mark the children born right after me, in the 1980s and 1990s. Some social scientists call us forty-year-olds "Xennials" because we're so close to the line. So if you are a millennial, let's just say we're peers. Anyway, in my heart I feel like I just left college.

### A Generation of Pioneering Problems

We whose ages currently span the twenties, thirties, forties, and fifties have more than the return of shoulder pads to lament. We're still working through the hard stuff that accompanied us as we came of age. We're dubbed the divorce generation because broken marriages peaked in 1980.[2] This

---

2. Susan Gregory Thomas, "The Divorce Generation," *Wall Street Journal,* July 9, 2011, https://www.wsj.com/articles/SB100014240527023035446045764 30341393583056.

divorce spree coincided with the sexual revolution.[3] As our parents liberated themselves from their marriages, they also found liberty in the new norms of casual relationships and alternative expressions of sexuality.

As the first latchkey generation, we found ourselves home alone, trying to figure out what was what and who was who. We grew up in uncertain times for sure.

## A Generation of Pioneering Promise

But the times were exciting too. In the United States we welcomed Title IX, a civil rights law that says no one can be excluded from any education program on the basis of gender. My girlfriends and I felt the effects of Title IX primarily in the sports world. Girls' sports began receiving more attention and funding, and we all found ourselves on the soccer field every afternoon, keeping up with the boys. Our coaches' and teachers' common refrain was, "Anything the boys can do, you can do better." My high school even had some hopeful female kickers for the boys' football team.

Sure, we were limping a little from our turbulent home lives. But our school days and social circles were full of possibility. "Be anything you want to be," people told us. Our only limit was our imaginations.

I was the editor in chief of my high school's newspaper during those potential-packed days. I recently found an old paper with an editorial written by yours truly. It was composed with no small amount of sass. The gist was this: the girls are filling the honors and AP (advanced placement)

3. Wikipedia, s.v. "Sexual revolution," last modified April 27, 2019, 6:49, https://en.wikipedia.org/w/index.php?title=Sexual_revolution&oldid=874901769/.

classrooms, but where are the boys? It was a celebration of Title IX. We girls really were advancing, beyond the boys even. At least in my context, we were gobbling up all the awards and scholarships and heading off to promising futures at the best colleges.

The world was cheering for us. We could feel it. "Girl power" was propelling us beyond where our mothers and grandmothers had ever been. We were determined to take the glass ceiling by storm—our sights were set on becoming CEOs, entrepreneurs, engineers, professors, lawyers, doctors, or, in my case, television broadcasters. Our predecessors were thrilled for us, and we didn't know any better.

With great confidence we set out into the women's world.

## You Can Do It!

The optimism of our mothers and the can-do spirit that washed over us girls shot us into adulthood. Some of us got degrees. Started careers. Found husbands. Had children. Filled important roles in our communities, in politics, and in churches.

You can have it all, they told us then and they keep telling us now. And we are certainly trying. Most of the women I know work (part time or full time or from home) or own their own businesses, volunteer, raise kids, participate in local sports and clubs, serve in their churches, work out, endeavor to put healthy food on the table, maintain active social lives, think global, shop local—and the list goes on. We are juggling laundry, promotions, car pools, and Sunday school. Girl power.

The cultural air we breathe fills us with optimism. And so we take deep breaths, and we keep running for the goal.

*Create your own destiny. You be you. Reach for the stars. You can be a self-made woman. You are in charge of your own happiness. You get what you give. Never let them see you sweat. Follow your dreams. Make it happen. You are enough.*

We're all reaching for that elusive gold star: becoming the women society says we can be. We keep pulling ourselves up by our bootstraps, guzzling our coffee, and looking in the mirror to remind ourselves, "You got this, sister. Go get 'em."

But then.

*Then.*

Almost without exception and as if on cue, we reach the end of ourselves. The coffee cup is empty. The self-talk grows quiet. We collapse on the couch. We are tired. This isn't working. Someone send help.

## We Did It! So Why Are We So Sad?

The feminist movement did indeed deliver better pay, equal rights, and more respect for us in many spheres of society. Today's women are indebted to the sisters who went before us. I am grateful for much of the fruit borne by women's liberation. Without those who came before me, I likely wouldn't be a student of culture and theology and writing this book.

But even as I celebrate the strong women of the past and present, I also wonder what's really going on. We Xennial women who shot out of the gates into adulthood with much promise and anticipation are not rejoicing the way I think our foremothers imagined we would.

It's not going according to plan. Being self-made women is wearing us out.

Researchers have found that "although women's life circumstances have improved greatly over the past few decades by most objective measures, their happiness has declined—both in absolute terms and relative to men's."[4]

In the United States, female mental and emotional health is in crisis. A Centers for Disease Control study reveals that in the last almost two decades, suicide rates among women have increased by 50 percent, and among girls ages ten to fourteen they have tripled.[5] We have to ask ourselves, *if things are supposed to be increasingly hopeful, why are we increasingly hopeless?*

Social scientists are divided on why women and girls are struggling. Some point to the fact that men still populate the highest paying jobs and the highest levels of elected office, and garner the most respect. Some blame sexual misconduct, as displayed so graphically in the #metoo movement. Many point out that while opportunities have been vastly opened outside the home for women, we still take care of everything inside the home; it's called the second shift, and it's primarily staffed by women. Some say it's just that we're too busy and nothing is getting the attention it deserves. Many believe social media plays a role.

## How Did We Get Here?

We have a map on our dining room table that our family loves to linger over after meals. Three-fourths of my daugh-

---

4. Sherrie Bourg Carter, "Meet the Least Happy People in America," *Psychology Today*, September 17, 2011, https://www.psychologytoday.com/us/blog/high -octane-women/201109/meet-the-least-happy-people-in-america.

5. Hilary Brueck, "The US Suicide Rate Has Increased 30% Since 2000—and It Tripled for Young Girls. Here's What We Can Do About It," *Business Insider*, June 14, 2018, https://www.businessinsider.com/us-suicide-rate-increased-since -2000-2018-6.

ters were born in Asia. After their childhoods there, we moved to Europe. We ended up back in the United States in time for their teen and young adult years. When we look at the map, we remember our favorite places in Japan and Thailand. We focus on the Czech Republic and remember our road trips through Europe.

We trace our fingers over three continents and remember how we got here, to Colorado. Each country plays an important role in who my daughters are right now. Those places are why fried rice and ramen are their comfort foods. They're why they love sushi and why Japanese curry and Czech goulash are treats in our home. The points on the journey reveal why they speak a second language and why they're still bewildered by American football and grocery stores and school supplies. Looking at that map and our shared history reminds us why we are who we are today and how we got here.

And so it is with this moment in global women's history. If we want to understand who we are today, we must trace our fingers along the map to find out how we got to this paradoxical moment of both great opportunity *and* great discouragement.

### Western Worldviews and Women

Our current condition is not just the overflow of the women's liberation movement or Title IX. It's not rooted solely in social media or the two-shift work many of us are doing. It's not simply the result of modern-day pitfalls and pressures.

Rather, we arrived here by following the natural progression of worldviews in the West over the last few hundred years. We're actually right where our path led us. Western worldviews brought us here, whether we realize it or not.

A worldview is exactly what it sounds like: it's how we, as a group—a family, a people group, a nation—view the world. Worldviews answer our big life questions: What is real? Who are we? How did we get here? Is there a god and if so, what is he or she like? What is the meaning of life? What should we be doing here? How do we know the difference between right and wrong? What happens when we die?

Worldviews are subtle. We breathe them in and out, usually without even knowing it. We take them for granted. They're our of-course-that's-the-way-things-are knee-jerk reactions. Unless you've spent time pondering why you think the way you do, it's likely that your worldview has developed without you really knowing it.

## A Quick Sprint through Worldviews

Stick with me here. Let's take a minute to trace the important worldviews from the past few hundred years, so we can have a better understanding of how we got here. Our worldview wasn't shaped in a vacuum. It's the culmination of influential thinkers and culture shapers. The thinkers below are our worldview ancestors; we may be tempted to think they have nothing to do with us, but they have played a major role in how you and I see the world in the twenty-first century.

### 1600s

Western philosophy really began back in the 1600s with the age of reason, fathered by René Descartes. He is famous for saying, "I think, therefore I am." This quote sums up the ideology of that time well: it's because of reason, or rationality, that we can know anything. Though subtle, this was the beginning of our looking to ourselves as the source of wisdom, of life, and of purpose.

### 1700s

The Enlightenment was quickly on Descartes's heels, with thinkers such as Swiss-born Jean-Jacques Rousseau. Rousseau is famous for rejecting anything that limited the freedom of self. He's the father of the if-it-feels-good-do-it movement. We are definitely living out the legacy of Rousseau's thinking today.

The 1700s was an age of revolution. Both the French and American revolutions threw off the shackles of church and state. With Rousseau, European and New World thinkers prioritized the individual above the institution.

### 1800s

The beginnings of the orientation toward self as authority in the 1600s and the rejection of church and state in the 1700s morphed into the modern philosophy of the 1800s. American Ralph Waldo Emerson triumphed self-reliance, saying, "Every one for himself; driven to find all his resources, hopes, rewards, society, and *deity* within himself."[6]

German philosopher Karl Marx also championed total autonomy. He said, "A being only considers himself independent when he stands on his own feet; and he only stands on his own feet when he *owes his existence to himself*."[7]

---

6. Ralph Waldo Emerson, *The Complete Works of Ralph Waldo Emerson: Lectures and Biographical Sketches*, ed. Edward Waldo Emerson (Boston: Houghton Mifflin, 1911), 329. Emphasis added.

7. Karl Marx and Frederick Engels, "Private Property and Communism," in *Collected Works*, vol. 3 (New York: International Publishers, 1975), 304, quoted

We know now that although many were wooed (and are still wooed) by Marx's promises of equity, his influence led to the self-deification of totalitarian leaders throughout the twentieth century. Applying his worldview to politics caused the death of millions throughout Russia, China, Cambodia, and elsewhere.

Charles Darwin convinced us that we evolved by chance and mutation, ultimately freeing us from any obligation to a creator or god outside of ourselves. Darwin, Marx, Emerson, and other thinkers from the 1800s led us to define our own reality; we will decide for ourselves how we got here, what our lives are for, and what's real.

### 1900s

The barely noticeable rise in the water that started in the 1600s with rationalism gained momentum throughout the 1700s with the rejection of the church and state and became a tidal wave in the 1800s with the elevation of self-reliance, self-existence, and self-deification. The tsunami wiped out our value for pursuing objective truth and carried us into the mid-1900s, landing us squarely in the existentialism movement. As the waters receded, the majority of us in the West set out to rebuild by defining our own meaning of life.

The varied definitions among us brought about postmodernism in the 1970s. Postmodernism says there is no metanarrative to life—in other words, there's no way to ultimately explain who we are or how we got here.[8] Post-

---

in Charles Colson and Nancy Pearcy, *How Now Shall We Live?* (Carol Stream, IL: Tyndale, 1999), 234, chap. 24, Kindle edition. Emphasis added.

8. This idea comes from Timothy Keller, *Making Sense of God: Finding God in the Modern World* (New York: Penguin, 2016), 200. Keller credits two sources in

modernism says any worldview that claims to interpret life and history through an overarching meaning is wrong (never mind that postmodernism itself attempts to interpret all of life with one overarching meaning, namely that there is no meaning).

And that's when we Jennifers, and Generation Xers, and millennials, and most likely you, dear reader, came on the scene.

You and I were born into an age that triumphed relativism and individualism. The culture of our childhoods was decidedly antiauthoritarian. Rather than *discovering* the objective truth, we were taught to *define* our own subjective truth. Unlike millennia of generations before us, we set out not to uncover the meaning of life, but to give our lives their own meaning.

## From Relying on Self to Deifying Self

Here in the 2000s, we've successfully thrown off the shackles of any institutionalized definition of truth or reality or right and wrong. We've triumphed freedom as our highest good.

Individual freedom trumps all former societal norms and values. It is ultimate.

Whether we knew it at the time or not, the priority and power of the individual were elevated in our elementary classrooms. The self-esteem movement of our childhoods utilized school curricula that taught us "to chant slogans like 'I can handle it,' 'I can make it happen,' and 'I am me,

---

his notes: Jean-Francois Lyotard, *The Postmodern Condition: A Report on Knowledge* (Minneapolis, MN: University of Minnesota Press, 1984), xxiv; and Richard Bauckham, "Reading Scripture as a Coherent Story," in *The Art of Reading Scripture*, ed. Richard B. Hays and Ellen F. Davis (Grand Rapids, MI: Eerdmans, 2003), 45.

I am enough.'"[9] The salvation of our childhood was found in ourselves. And we carried it into adulthood.

Look no further than Instagram and home decor stores to see the very same messages on our coffee cups and throw pillows. We see this prioritizing of self in popular culture, television and movies, parenting books, music—it's everywhere.

We've consecrated self not just in pop culture, but in our laws too. In 1992, the Supreme Court "enshrined this view in law when it opined 'the heart of liberty' is to 'define one's own concept of existence, of the meaning of the universe.'"[10] Defining one's own reality is upheld in all manner of policies on university campuses, in business boardrooms, and on public bathroom signs.

Nothing is allowed to get in the way of you being you. You define you. You do you. All other societal scaffolding must submit to self, our greatest value.

## Fragility: The Primary Problem with Deifying Self

When we deify ourselves, we require reality to conform to our own desires, rather than the other way around (conforming ourselves to reality). And whether we know it or not, this self-deification requires us to worship ourselves, to uphold ourselves, to convince ourselves that we are enough and worthy of following.

When we become our own source of meaning, we also become our only source of satisfaction and fulfillment. We set ourselves in a cycle of defining ourselves and worshiping ourselves.

---

9. Colson and Pearcey, *How Now Shall We Live?*, 267.
10. Timothy Keller, *The Reason for God: Belief in an Age of Skepticism* (New York: Penguin, 2008), 47.

To uphold this worldview, we must become our own masters. Ironically, we don't actually become free. We must not only muster our own meaning and goals and dreams, but we must supply our own energy and ability to accomplish them. With ourselves on the throne we must truly be self-made women: we must conjure up everything from the meaning of life to the energy and ability to live it out.

This makes us fragile. It's all on us. Today we have to create our worlds and make them go round too.

## Disability: When the Deified Self Is Not Enough

The problem with self-deification is that it limits oneself to oneself. We disable ourselves by not permitting ourselves to look to something bigger—something outside (or *someone* outside, as we'll investigate in the next chapter)—for our meaning and purpose. Our only hope is to believe ourselves when we say we are enough.

And we must eat a steady diet of the praise of others. How do you know you've arrived at being *anything you want to be* if you don't receive accolades for your achievements? A ho-hum life is not enough to know that you're at the pinnacle of your dreams. We've got to be out there, receiving the applause of the multitudes.

But the appetite for approval is insatiable. And we're never quite sure we're on track. How many "likes" on social media is enough to know that you've finally reached the stars?

The self-esteem mantras of our childhood eventually ring hollow. The "I can make it happen" slogan repeated by our teachers, parents, pop culture, and even the law of the land doesn't give us the life we thought it would. Ironically, the worldview that is supposed to give us life sucks it right out of us.

If you and I cannot be who we set out to be, then we've lost ourselves. As pastor and author Timothy Keller says, "The modern self is crushing."[11] Following our hearts doesn't work when our hearts must also be the source of where we're going and how to get there. We're like a dog chasing its tail. There's no beginning. There's no outside source for the needed energy and joy and direction we're trying to go.

And so we end up chasing our tails frantically until we're exhausted. As we trace the map of historical world-views, we see that the path that has led us to triumph self above all has also led us to our own destruction.

We are destroying ourselves by trying to follow ourselves.

Since the latter half of the twentieth century, we have assumed that we have the authority to create ourselves and live out our own reality. But this view is fatally flawed. It's what's ailing my generation and yours.

## We Are in the ER, and We Need an Accurate Diagnosis

At one point in my early parenting years, I had three daughters ages three and under. Whatever madness you're picturing is accurate. During that season of crazy I got a sore throat that wouldn't let go. I was downing Advil multiple times a day to keep the soreness, swelling, and fever at bay. But after a few days, the swelling got to the point that I was having trouble breathing. So I did what any mom of young children would do: *I drove myself* to the emergency room. It was simply easier to leave the kids at home with

---

11. Keller, *Making Sense of God*, 134.

my husband than to have him drive the whole family to the hospital.

I parked my car and went inside the ER expecting to wait for hours to be seen. Instead, after answering a few questions, I was whisked behind a curtain and started receiving treatment. The doctor on duty was clearly alarmed.

I heard her call my husband, "Sir, your wife is very sick. She won't be home anytime soon. We'll be giving her intravenous antibiotics and possibly inserting a trach tube. She'll be in ICU, so come down here when you can." I got morphine for the pain and slipped in and out of awareness of my surroundings for the next few days.

Clearly, I had misdiagnosed my sore throat. What initially felt like a small hassle grew and grew until it was actually a life-threatening crisis. The Advil wasn't going to cut it. What I thought was a cold was actually an aggressive infection closing my throat. My uneducated misdiagnosis put my family and me in peril.

A misdiagnosis for understanding the current mental and emotional health crisis for women in the West will do the same thing. We cannot simply pop a few Advil if we're going to have any hope of coming out of this crash we're in.

It's not that the feminist movement had it all wrong. It's not that we women are just doing too much and we're tired. It's not that mental health medicine and practitioners aren't helpful. It's that our problem is deep down. *It's soul deep.*

Author Rosaria Butterfield nails it when she writes, "The real issue at the core is personhood. Failing to discern rightly who we are renders us unable to accurately discern anything we touch, feel, think, or dream. Failing to discern rightly who we are renders us unable to properly know who God is. We are truly lost in a darkness of our own making."[12]

The bold theologian and Reformer John Calvin called it five hundred years ago when he said, "For the plague of submitting to our own rule leads us straight to ruin."[13] Truly, we are lost in a darkness of our own making, and we got here by dethroning God and enthroning ourselves.

We've deified ourselves. And it's led to our demise.

## The Remedy: Remembering Who We Are and Whose We Are

Culture tells us the remedy for our burnout is more me-time. What we need is more rest. More quiet times alone. A nicer luxury vehicle that can block out the stress of the world. Possibly a nanny and a cleaning lady to help us balance it all. More wine. More coffee. Therapy, medicine. More self-talk. Get your tribe, get your people, get your momfia to remind you that you are enough and you can do this.

But I propose that we need to go way back to the beginning. We need to remember *who we are and whose we are.* How were we created and by whom? For what purpose were we designed? On what kind of energy are we meant to run?

Our remedy is in reclaiming our worldview. It's in rejecting the self-help movement that birthed us and in reorienting ourselves back toward the God who made us. Healing must happen in our souls. Our health will come when we root ourselves in what's true.

Let's face it: we were duped by the culture that raised us. The ideas that we swim around in are wreaking havoc. As

12. Rosaria Butterfield, *The Gospel Comes with a House Key: Practicing Radically Ordinary Hospitality in Our Post-Christian World* (Wheaton, IL: Crossway, 2018), 48.
13. John Calvin, *A Little Book on the Christian Life,* trans. Aaron Denlinger and Burk Parsons (Sanford, FL: Reformation Trust, 2017), 22–23.

we match them up against the biblical truths of the gospel, we see how they ring hollow.

Like the alluring but destructive creatures in Greek mythology, self is a Siren. We are indeed attracted to ourselves. But rooting ourselves in ourselves has led to our ruin. The I-can-do-this self-talk and building ourselves up from the inside has exhausted us. We see now that there is no rest for the one who depends on herself for everything.

Our current crisis condition is not what the giver of life intended. He created us in a specific way, for a specific purpose. And he intended that we be energized and filled with joy in a relationship with him.

Let's admit that we are not enough, and turn to the God who is.

## Questions for Personal Reflection or Group Discussion

1. What are some of the unspoken worldviews you were born into?

2. What worldview ideas from the 1600s, 1700s, 1800s, or 1900s do you see playing out in culture today?

3. What problems do you see with self-help?

4.  Think about our cultural trend to define reality, rather than discover reality. In other words, we tend to require reality to conform to our own desires, rather than the other way around (conforming ourselves to reality). What are some real-life examples where this is problematic?

5.  Do you agree that "the modern self is crushing"? Reflect on the cycle required by self-deification: we must worship ourselves, to uphold ourselves, to convince ourselves that we are enough and worthy of following. Have you experienced this?

6.  Read Colossians 2:8 and Romans 1:28–30. How do these verses speak to our current culture?

7.  Ask God to reveal where you have been conformed to the culture's ideals rather than to God's ideals. Where have you given over your mind, and where do you need to be renewed? Meditate on Romans 15:13, and ask God to reveal himself to you and to show you where to find lasting joy as make your way through this book.

# 2

# What the Giver of Life Intended

When my husband turned forty, we were living in Europe. I planned an elaborate surprise weekend for just the two of us: forty-eight hours in Florence for his fortieth. Adding to the festivities (and apparently to the alliteration), I solicited our family in the States to see if they'd like to contribute to the icing on the cake: a Ferrari.

Not a Ferrari *for* him. But a chance for him to drive one, albeit briefly. I knew it would be the crowning glory of our weekend. What a memory! What photos! What an I'm-turning-forty thing to do!

Mark had no idea what was coming. We set out to sightsee, and I led us up to the Piazzale Michelangelo, to the meeting point for the drive. There, overlooking the city, with the Duomo and Ponte Vecchio in the distance, sat a shiny red convertible 488 Spider. Mark's eyes and mouth grew wide when I identified ourselves to the Ferrari guy. It was priceless.

For a minute.

The Ferrari fete first began to fizzle when the guy motioned for all three of us to get in. As in, he would be going with us. As in, no, you don't get to take this baby out on the open road without a babysitter.

Mark remained upbeat while I folded my six-foot frame into the one-foot space some would call a back seat. The Ferrari started with a roar. Mark adjusted his sunglasses, smiled at me in the rearview mirror, and carefully wove his way beyond the crowds and street vendors in anticipation of the Italian countryside.

Except we never got there.

I had imagined that the money our family pooled for the occasion had bought twenty minutes of Ferrari bliss. Instead, for twenty minutes Mark shifted in and out of first gear—sometimes second, but rarely—as we sat in Italian traffic. The rearview looks went from eager anticipation to sober realization to downright dissipation.

Holding on to hope, Mark asked about the silver button on the dashboard that read *Launch*. "Never, ever touch that," the babysitter said. Both car and driver withered.

The Ferrari was designed for one thing: speed. This slow jaunt around the city was not what the makers had in mind. The thundering engine, the silver launch button, all six gears, and the rear-wheel drive begged for acceleration.

I'm no car guy, but it was clear in that moment that "the finest race-developed technological solutions with the joy of en plein air driving [meant] to deliver an exhilarating experience behind the wheel" would not be.[1] The marvel-

1. "The Prancing Horse's Best Ever Open-Top Performance," Ferrari website, https://auto.ferrari.com/en_US/sports-cars-models/car-range/ferrari-488-pista -spider/, accessed December 27, 2018.

ous machine would not be doing what it was made to do. It failed to launch.

In the same way, when you and I live in ways that our Maker does not intend, we suffer. We languish when our purpose goes unrealized. Like the Ferrari, we groan and idle and make slow progress, but never take off. We never soar, reach full speed, or flourish at our fullest potential.

As the race car was made for speed, you and I were made for God. He is our Maker. He designed us for himself.

We were made by God and for God.

## What's Our Story?

As twenty-first-century humans, we are quick to wonder what we should be *doing*. We are inundated with options for education, hobbies, free time, passions to fulfill, causes to lobby, justice issues to champion. We want to know *how* to spend ourselves, our resources, our future. We prioritize action.

But before you and I can figure out what we should be doing, we need to know *of what story* we're a part.[2] How can we know what to do if we don't know our context? What's the larger plot around us? Who's the author? And where in the story did he write us in?

The Bible is the story of God, and we, his creatures, are featured there too.

Certainly outside the church, and sadly, quite often inside the church, the Bible is viewed as a good book full of pithy wisdom. We treat it like Christian fortune cookies—

---

2. Alasdair MacIntyre, *After Virtue: A Study in Moral Theory*, 2nd ed. (Notre Dame, FR: University of Notre Dame Press, 1984), 216, as quoted in James K. A. Smith, *You Are What You Love: The Spiritual Power of Habit* (Grand Rapids, MI: Brazos Press, 2016), 89.

a bunch of fragments with some good ideas that may or may not have anything to do with us. Popular culture pats the Bible on its head: it's nice, but it's ancient literature, outdated, irrelevant.

But the story of Scripture is preeminent. It is from everlasting to everlasting. It is the final reality, the ultimate truth of all time. It's the story that we fit into. And that last detail is especially important for us today: *we fit into the story*. It's not *the story that we fit into us*, when convenient.

We are story people. We naturally want to make sense of who we are, where we've come from, and where we're going. One Bible scholar gives a timely warning: "Because we ourselves are 'relentlessly narratival,' if we don't get our story from the Bible, we will end up fitting pieces of the Bible into a story we've picked up from somewhere else. We have no choice but to live our lives as a narrative that fits into some bigger narrative that we believe makes sense of the world."[3]

We are "relentlessly narratival." And so, to rightly understand our own story, we must come to the Bible for what it is: one unified drama—a metanarrative, a grand story that explains *everything*.

## The Big Story of the Bible

While the Bible contains sixty-six books, written over the span of 1,500 years by forty authors in three languages, it actually contains one unified story: "From Genesis to Revelation, the Bible is telling us about the reign and rule of God."[4]

---

3. Glenn Paauw, *Saving the Bible from Ourselves: Learning to Read and Live the Bible Well* (Downer's Grove, IL: InterVarsity Press, 2016), chap. 7, Kindle edition.
4. Jen Wilkin, *Women of the Word: How to Study the Bible with Both Our Hearts and Our Minds* (Wheaton, IL: Crossway, 2014), 50.

The big story of the Bible is made up of four major movements: creation, fall, redemption, and restoration. Simply put, creation is how we came to be on this planet, the fall is when we originally sinned and rebelled against God, redemption is when Jesus came and paid the punishment for our sins on our behalf, and restoration is what's coming in the future when God will make all things new on earth and in heaven.

If we were to look at an eternal timeline, the words "You Are Here" would be marked in red between the two movements of redemption and restoration. That's where you and I are right now. Humanity has already lived through creation and the fall. And while redemption has already come in Christ, restoration is not yet here.

For our purposes in this chapter, we're most concerned with the first movement in the big story of the Bible: creation. By going back to the beginning we can better understand why we're in the state we're in right now.

Our origins can actually tell us why women are so disillusioned today, in the twenty-first century.

## Created on Purpose for a Purpose: In His Image and for His Glory

Creation is hotly debated because it has enormous ramifications. If it's true that we have a Creator and we're not here by chance, then we have to look to him to answer our big questions. The "most important implication of creation is that it gives us our basic understanding of who we are; our view of origins determines our view of human nature."[5]

---

5. Charles Colson and Nancy Pearcy, *How Now Shall We Live?* (Carol Stream, IL: Tyndale, 1999), 140, Kindle edition.

You would be hard-pressed to find a native English speaker who doesn't know where to find the words "In the beginning, God created" (Gen. 1:1). Though they may not be unanimously believed, they are ubiquitously known to be the opening words of the Bible. Twenty-seven verses after "in the beginning"—after God created the heavens and the earth, day and night, the sky and water, plants and trees, the sun, moon, and stars, fish and birds, and livestock, creeping things, and beasts—God "created man in his own image, in the image of God he created him; male and female he created them" (Gen. 1:27).

You and I were created by God and in his image. The psalmist said, "Know that the LORD, he is God! / It is he who made us, and we are his; / we are his people . . ." (Ps. 100:3).

If we came from God, then not only do we owe our existence to God, but it is God alone who can tell us why we're here, what will hurt us, and how to thrive. The storywriter is also the storyteller. He wrote us into the story, and he can tell us about ourselves—he has the answers.

This might seem obvious, but you and I are not like trees and flowers and dogs and cats and elephants. We reflect God. Of course only God is perfect; only he can be fully loving and just and patient and kind. But we too bear these attributes. Though not without fault, you and I can be creative, wise, truthful, merciful, good, and many other things that God is.

Because all humans everywhere are made in God's image, all humans everywhere have immeasurable value. This truth is why Christians are (or should be) so passionate about life issues: abortion and euthanasia and everything in between, helping refugees, fighting racism, alleviating poverty, making education accessible, and providing parents to orphans across the globe. We are driven to care for one another because of God's image in all of us. We are not like the birds and bees and begonias and belugas.

The Creator of the universe created you and me on purpose and for a purpose. As Colossians 1:16 says, "For by him all things were created . . . all things were created through him and for him." We were made by God and for God. We were made in his image to reflect his image.

## Created by Him: Designed to Be Fueled by God

The words of Colossians 1:15–20 are all-encompassing. Paul says all things were created by Jesus, for Jesus, and through Jesus, and that he is before all things and holds everything together. Not only is he the Creator and sustainer of our lives, but he's also our fuel.

Knowing and making the right fuel choice is vital if we, or any organism or machine, are to run well. Fuel choice is so important, in fact, that I cannot go to fill up my car without some trepidation. Even back here in the States, where I first learned to drive, the gas station makes me anxious.

Where I've lived, the fuel labels aren't often in English, and there are usually four or five choices to pick from. Accidentally fueling a diesel car with unleaded or an unleaded car with diesel creates huge problems. We've had more than one friend suffer roadside breakdowns and significant engine damage after making the wrong choice. Every time I fuel up, I wrestle with the fear that I'm going to ruin our family car.

The analogy here is clear. Fuel matters. Not just for cars, but for you and me as well. Our Creator, our giver of life, intended that we would live in relationship with him forever. He is to be our fuel.

In his well-loved book, *Mere Christianity*, author C. S. Lewis said, "God designed the human machine to run on Himself. He Himself is the fuel our spirits were designed to burn, or the food our spirits were designed to feed on. There is no other. That is why it is just no good asking God to make us happy in our own way."[6]

About 1,500 years before C. S. Lewis, the early church father Augustine put it another way: "You have made us for yourself, and our heart is restless until it rests in you."[7]

Jesus spoke of our relationship with him in terms of *abiding*, meaning to stay or reside. He said, "Abide in me, and I in you . . . apart from me you can do nothing" (John 15:4–5). The giver of life also intends to be the sustainer of life, in an eternal relationship with us humans, his unique and special creatures.

We twenty-first-century women have been running on ourselves, rather than our God. We've been running on self-help, self-empowerment, and self-actualization. The fuel of self has run out, and that's why we're tired and discouraged and even in crisis.

Enough about me. And enough about you. If we want to keep running, we need to run on the fuel we're made for—God himself. We will indeed be restless until then.

## Created for Him: Designed to Glorify God

The Bible says that not only were we created by God, but also that we were created *for* God. We were made for his

6. C. S. Lewis, *Mere Christianity* (New York: Harper Collins, 1952), 50.

7. Augustine, *Confessions*, trans. Henry Chadwick (Oxford: Oxford University Press, 1992), 1.1.1, as quoted in Smith, *You Are What You Love*, 8.

glory. As the prophet Isaiah said, "Bring my sons from afar / and my daughters from the end of the earth, / everyone who is called by my name, / whom I created for my glory, / whom I formed and made" (Isa. 43:6–7).

To live for God's glory is to live in such a way as to display him. It's a way of living that honors God and shows the world who he is and what he's like. Those of us who know him are called to reveal him to others.

We weren't made to glorify ourselves, but to glorify our Maker. Jesus was clear about this in the Sermon on the Mount: "Let your light shine before others, so that they may see your good works and give glory to your Father who is in heaven" (Matt. 5:16).

God made us to be light makers, and the spotlight is meant to shine right back on him.

The apostle Paul said, "We are his workmanship, created in Christ Jesus for good works, which God prepared beforehand, that we should walk in them" (Eph. 2:10). The work that is in our lives was put there by God. And we are to work unto him. There's purpose in our toil—a reason for our highs and lows.

If you ever wonder what on earth you are here for, there is a very good answer. God made you on purpose and for a purpose. You are meant to abide in him, to be in relationship with him. You bear his image, and he wants you to reflect him to others. You are not merely clocking in at your job, changing diapers, going to school, climbing the corporate ladder, attending PTA, or going through the motions for no good reason. You and I are in our specific roles to become more like our Maker and to reveal him to a watching world.

It's like this: My three brown-eyed biological daughters have such dark eyes that you cannot discern their irises from their pupils. Their eyes are from their dad, whose Italian heritage is undeniable. My eyes, on the other hand, are blue, so when people see my daughters, they see my husband, not me. There is no mistaking that they belong to him.

That is our purpose too—to look like our Father. To be unmistakably like him. We are to "be imitators of God, as beloved children" (Eph. 5:1). Our Father is the giver of life. As our lives point others back to him, we point them to their source and the fuel by which they can live and thrive.

## The Fall: When We First Believed We Could Be Like God

The Siren call of self is as old as we humans. Satan's favorite question was his first question, *Did God really say that?* (Gen. 3:1). The serpent wanted to sow seeds of doubt in Adam and Eve that God had their best interests in mind. His aim was to cause the first humans to wonder if God was holding out on them, if they didn't deserve better than what he was providing.

The serpent told Eve, *You won't die if you eat the fruit of that tree; you'll just be like God. You have nothing to worry about. Don't you want to be like God? Go ahead and take a bite* (Gen. 3:4–5).

When the first humans fell for the serpent's lie in the beginning of Genesis 3, God's image in us was marred. Life in the garden, life in constant communion with our Creator, ended.

We believed then and we still believe now that we can be like God. Lewis wrote:

What Satan put into the heads of our remote ancestors was the idea that they could 'be like gods'—could set up on their own as if they had created themselves—be their own masters—invent some sort of happiness for themselves outside God, apart from God. And out of that hopeless attempt has come . . . the long terrible story of man trying to find something other than God which will make him happy"[8]

That's where many of us are today. We are stuck in the fall. We haven't moved beyond our belief that we can be our own god. God's image in us has been marred to the point that we don't believe we ever bore it in the first place.

The question we have to get at, though, is this: *Is this who I really am?* Or, as Rosaria Butterfield writes, "Is it how the fall of Adam made me? Is it my authentic identity or the distorted one that came through the power of Adam's . . . sin to render my deep and primal feelings untrustworthy and untrue?"[9]

In other words, is this fallen person *who* I am or *how* I am?[10]

Am I more than an impatient mom? More than a prideful worker? More than a coveter of my neighbor's good things? More than an adulterer? More than a liar? More than a murderer? More than an angry wife or daughter or sister? Are those sins that define me, or are they sins that distract me from who I'm created and redeemed to be?

The fall brought sin nature into our lives, but we weren't originally created that way. Redemption builds a bridge back to what God intended, and we'll fully arrive there one day when he brings about restoration.

---

8. Lewis, *Mere Christianity*, 49.
9. Rosaria Butterfield, *The Gospel Comes with a House Key: Practicing Radically Ordinary Hospitality in Our Post-Christian World* (Wheaton, IL: Crossway, 2018), 50.
10. Butterfield, *The Gospel Comes with a House Key*, 51.

## Redemption: God Makes a Way

God's grace—redemption—appears right after the fall. In Genesis 3:15 God promises a future salvation that will come through Jesus, who will bruise the head of Satan, defeating him forever.

Know this: God is not only our Creator, but he's also our Redeemer. He gave us life, and when we rebelled, he stepped in to save us. He is author and rescuer and Maker and Savior. We'll explore this immeasurably good news more in the next chapter.

## Restoration: Paradise Lost Will Be Restored

Did you know our current, fallen, broken-down world is not all that will be? Heaven and earth will be restored. Randy Alcorn, in his book *Heaven*, calls this lifetime the *beforelife*. Our so-called *afterlife* is *the* life we're all waiting for.[11] This is just the pre-party, friends.

This life is not all there is. Part of being made in God's image means that we will live forever. Paradise lost will be restored.

The apostle John wrote about our future hope: "Behold, the dwelling place of God is with man. . . . God himself will be with them as their God. He will wipe away every tear from their eyes, and death shall be no more. . . . And he who was seated on the throne said, 'Behold, I am making all things new'" (Rev. 21:3–5).

We feel this in our bones, don't we? We know deep down that this isn't it. We know something has been lost that must be restored. Our hunch is right. Let's live in light of that reality.

---

11. Randy Alcorn, *Heaven* (Carol Stream, IL: Tyndale, 2004), 415.

These four movements make up the big story of the Bible. God created us, we rebelled against him, he redeemed us, and one day all will be restored. That big story about God is also our story because we were made in his image.

We must know that we're a part of that story before we can know what we must do. It's in tethering ourselves to that story—in recognizing that we were created on purpose for a purpose—that we will thrive.

God says, *I made you in my image to live for my glory*. Culture says, *Be self-made in whatever image you like and live for your own glory*. This is a counterfeit calling, and it's killing us.

## Communion with the Divine Gives Joy

My family and friends know me for something I say almost daily. Being a Colorado native and a lover of the mountains, I am known for exclaiming, "Feast your eyes, children!"

Whether we're on the highway or in the middle of doing yard work, the beauty of the Rocky Mountains stops me in my tracks all the time. I just have to say it. And now the people in my life say it to one another.

The exclamation has caught on in our community because of what it points to. It's not just that the purple mountains' majesty is nice to look at. It's that those mountains make us feel small, and they point to something—someone—big. They profess their Maker. They proclaim that God is powerful and huge and able. If he can make them, then he can hold us in his hands. Even the mountains, seemingly just big rocks, point beyond themselves.

You and I want to live beyond ourselves, don't we? We crave a purpose and a power that's bigger than us, participating in something that really matters. We were made for transcendence. We were made to desire meaning that surpasses our lifetimes and exceeds our own limits.

Reflecting on our natural bent for transcendence, Tim Keller hearkens back to the words of Augustine: "Whether we acknowledge God or not, since we were created for it, we will always look for the infinite joy we were designed to find in loving communion with the Divine."[12]

Did you catch that? We were designed to find joy in loving communion with the Divine.

We find joy when we invest in our relationship with God, when we acknowledge that we have a Maker, and when we seek to live for his glory. In both life's highs and life's lows, when we acknowledge where we came from and what we're here for, he gives us joy.

Perhaps you sense this during life's sweet highs. Maybe you feel joy when you look out at the ocean, or when you see your baby smile, or when you connect deeply with another human from a completely different background, or when you behold the crazy colors at the aquarium, or when you walk down the aisle on your wedding day. That joy is deep because it transcends us. It connects us to the God who made us and who made the very thing we're experiencing.

It's easy to suspect that God is present and good, a kind Creator who remains connected to us when we experience life's highs. But he's there in the lows too. I think of Corrie and Betsie ten Boom. Corrie and Betsie were Christians in the Netherlands when the Nazis swept through Europe, imprisoning and exterminating Jews and others considered undesirable. Along with their father, the ten Boom sisters

---

12. Augustine, *The City of God*, trans. Henry Bettenson (London: Penguin Books, 1972), 637 (book 15, chap. 23), as quoted in Keller, *Making Sense of God*, 90.

hid Jews in their home and were ultimately found out and sent to the deadly Ravensbrück concentration camp.

In *The Hiding Place*, Corrie wrote about Betsie's abiding joy in God, even amid their horrific trials.[13] She recounts that one night Betsie took the words of Scripture to heart. She believed that even in a death camp, they must "rejoice always" and "give thanks in all circumstances" (1 Thess. 5:16, 18). So Betsie prayed and thanked God for everything she could think of: that she and Corrie were together, that they had a forbidden Bible with them, that other women could hear them read the Bible, and finally for the fleas that had stricken them.

Not surprisingly, Corrie was horrified that her sister thanked God for the fleas. But Betsie believed that even the fleas pointed to their Maker and had a purpose. Indeed they did. The women later learned that the presence of fleas kept the Nazi guards from entering their barracks, for fear of being plagued with fleas themselves. And so the women were able to continue reading the Bible and sharing God's love with one another.

It's not only historical heroes of the faith who experience God's nearness in pain. My own mother-in-law was ravaged by ALS (also known as Lou Gehrig's disease) over the course of three years. As she lay dying, wracked by unspeakable pain that her medicine could no longer lessen, she told my husband, her son, that she wouldn't change a thing. She had been so ministered to by the Lord, she had so felt his presence and peace in her hour of need, that she wouldn't have given ALS back if she could have.

---

13. Corrie ten Boom, *The Hiding Place* (Grand Rapids, MI: Chosen Books, 1971), 209.

Likewise, our dear friend Doug graduated to heaven at a young age because of fast-moving cancer. He left behind a wife, five children adopted from foster care, and one young and unexpected biological son. Before he died, Doug's family sat in the crowd as he delivered a sermon, testifying to God's goodness in the midst of his sickness. I wrote his words in the margin of my Bible: "I know I've been healed already. With that in my back pocket, I can do whatever God asks me." Though very sick, Doug lived—thrived even!—from his relationship with his Maker.

Many of life's hard lows aren't as poignant as ALS and cancer. They are slow and grating. The complicated marriage, the thankless and mundane work, the arduous adoption journey, the unexpected job loss. But these too are opportunities for unexpected joy. When we take on such tasks by abiding in the Lord, by staying connected to him, he gives fuel and contentment—and yes, even joy—when we least expect it. We'll explore this lasting joy further in chapters 6 and 7. When we are fueled by God and seek to honor him in the midst of what's hard, he is known to deliver deep joy.

Both life's highs and life's lows point us to our Creator. Majesty and beauty, as well as pain and hardship, remind us that we are transcendent beings. We are part of a story that exceeds our own.

N. T. Wright says that when we wonder, "What are we here for in the first place? The fundamental answer . . . is that what we're 'here for' is to become genuine human beings, reflecting the God in whose image we're made."[14] To

---

14. N. T. Wright, *After You Believe: Why Christian Character Matters* (San Francisco: HarperOne, 2012), 25, as quoted in Smith, *You Are What You Love*, 87–88.

be our truest selves, to walk in our most genuine identity, does not come from within. Rather it comes from being fueled by our relationship with God and living for his glory. As creatures designed by him and for him, this is our best and truest self. To live any other way is to invite our downfall.

## Let's Return to Our Author

On our own, we are precarious. Our lives are fragile and dependent on the undergirding of forces we cannot control. But the truth is, we are part of a great—the greatest—story.

We are not dislocated, maverick beings who must conjure up our own purpose and power. And that's wonderful news! We belong to someone, and he's busy doing something in and through each of us.

The truth that we are dependent beings, that we were made by God and for God, is liberating. When I realize that my life is not my own, that it is by and for my very capable Maker, I no longer have to clamor to create my own success. It is not on me to make myself great. I'm in his hands. And he's already the greatest.

Because of the fall, we want to depend wholly on ourselves, but God says, *Come to me*. We must return to our Maker and acknowledge that our life and breath and everything else come from him—and that's a good thing. This news is not limiting or an obstacle to our thriving. It's the very key to our boundless joy. As Augustine said, our hearts will be restless until they find rest in God.

Let's return to our Creator, our author. We were made for him and by him, and we're called to live in relationship with him. You and I will never thrive merely as *who* we are; we must know and live from the truth of *whose* we are.

## Questions for Personal or Group Reflection

1. Who is the Bible primarily about? What is the big story of the Bible? What are the four major movements of the big story of the Bible?

2. What are some of life's highs that have pointed you back to your Creator? What are some of life's lows that have pointed you back to your Creator?

3. Do you agree or disagree that you can only find lasting joy in relationship with the Divine?

4. Have you experienced burnout from trying to run on the fuel of self—from living as if you were your own Maker and seeking to give yourself glory? Read John 15:4–5 and reflect on what it would mean for you to daily abide in Jesus.

5. What are some practical ways you can give glory to God in your own life?

6. Does your sinful, fallen behavior define you? Or is your identity rooted in who you were created and redeemed to be? Why does this distinction matter?

7. Think about and respond to Augustine's belief that our hearts are restless until they find rest in God. Are you at rest?

8. Read Psalm 16 and meditate especially on verse 11. How is this different from the wisdom of the world? Ask the Lord to help you continually pursue the true path of life.

**3**

# Rooted in Christ

Beginning in 2004, my family lived on a subtropical island for about ten years. As natives of the high desert in Colorado, my husband and I were not prepared to cultivate the jungle that was our yard. And by cultivate I mean hack back the greenery that constantly threatened to take over our home. Little effort was required to enjoy year-round hibiscus, thick green grass, flowering oleander, and a mulberry tree in the front yard. But much effort was required if we wanted to maintain a clear path to our front door or to keep vines from growing over our windows. Our best lawn tools were machetes, which we routinely wielded.

One of the most prolific trees on our island was the banyan tree. The banyan is easily recognizable because of the roots that grow out from the trees' high branches and then reach deep into the ground. Have you ever seen a tree that grows roots from up high? The roots come down from all sides. And not just a few roots—enough to create a sort of cage around the tree's trunk.

As toddlers and young children, my kids loved to play inside the banyans. The above-ground roots made a magical play place, a little kingdom where they could play pretend. While children may love banyans, anyone wanting to maintain their property feels exactly opposite. Daily, gardeners—covered by protective clothing from head to toe—whack away at the roots, attempting to maintain separation between the ground and the top of the tree.

Each root that hangs from the banyan's branch is actually a new tree. It is evidence of a seed that nestled into a crevice of one of the tree's branches. Because of the moisture available in the tree and in the air, that little seed easily grows roots and shoots them down to the ground, in an attempt to establish itself as its own, new tree. If someone doesn't whack away those roots, banyans will multiply and create a dense, impenetrable jungle.

The soil in the subtropics is rich and red and always moist. The nutrient-rich land supports a lavish banyan jungle, no problem. But back here in Colorado my husband and I look over our backyard with fledgling brownish grass and shake our heads. We fertilize. We aerate. We water constantly. We try with all our might to create the lush green lawn pictured on the bags of the good soil we bought. But the reality is roots have a tough time finding a home in our desert-dry soil.

### Roots Matter, Soil Matters

Plants must be rooted in order to live. And the soil must be just right if they're going to thrive. Roots matter. Soil matters. Without the right kind of soil, roots die and plants perish.

And so it is with us humans and our fragile lives. Without deep roots in the right kind of soil, we perish.

Several years before our island adventure, when I found myself on the floor of my college dorm room, unable to bounce back, I was withering. My roots were unable to support me because they were seeking nourishment in the wrong soil. The roots of my soul could not grow deep into the nourishment of my Creator and Savior because the soil wasn't good. It was contaminated.

While there were good things there—I did believe in God, and I had even made a profession of faith in Jesus as my Savior when I was eleven years old—the truth was overpowered by many toxins. My soul needed pure soil, not the duplicity in which I had been living.

It took a crisis, a coming to the end of myself, an outright debilitation, for me to realize that my current way of life was not sustainable.

## Divided

I grew up divided. My parents divorced when I was eight, and my time was divided between them until I went to college. One week with my mom and one week with my dad. My ambitions were also divided. Work hard and play hard. I wanted good grades and leadership roles, but also social credibility. Even my fledgling spiritual life was divided. I went to church when there wasn't something more socially pressing to do. Following the wisdom of the world, I kept my options open.

That lifestyle worked for a long time. I look back on my childhood and teen years with fondness. Those were fun days. But they were numbered. God, in his mercy, caused those divided goals to eventually ring hollow. I was not aware of my shifting emotions until I was in a heap on my dorm room floor. The academic and social successes I had enjoyed were not delivering the high I was accustomed to.

My eyes were being opened to the futility of my divided life for the first time. My feet were in two worlds. One foot sprinted after accolades, titles, a dream job, future wealth, and fame. The other foot sort of strolled in and out of church with some idea that God mattered, but unconvinced that he mattered more than what the world had to offer.

I didn't know Jesus's words at the time, but they were playing out in my own life: "If a house is divided against itself, that house will not be able to stand" (Mark 3:25). My divided life was crumbling around me. God allowed my worldly endeavors to prove themselves bankrupt, that I might cry out to him and find him.

I was mixing the sweet soil of my Savior with the toxic soil of the world's wisdom and my own selfish pursuits. It was really a "duplicity of heart."[1] I wanted some of what Jesus has to offer—some nutrients and good stuff to get me through—but not so much that I wanted God to purify the soil and enable me to prioritize his will over worldly pleasures.

I was the benign American Christian. As Tim Keller points out, most Americans tend to think "the best kind of Christian would be someone in the middle, someone who doesn't go all the way with it, who believes it, but is not devoted to it."[2] We want just enough faith to make us good, moral people, *on the right side of history*, as we love

---

1. John Calvin, *A Little Book on the Christian Life*, trans. Aaron Denlinger and Burk Parsons (Sanford, FL: Reformation Trust, 2017), 16.
2. Timothy Keller, *The Reason for God: Belief in an Age of Skepticism* (New York: Penguin, 2008), 57.

to say. But we don't want to be fanatics—people assigned to the fringe—those who actually believe the Bible and live according to it. Popular opinion tells us those people are weird and extreme, and their options for lifestyle and wealth and status are limited by the prohibitions of God.

But Jesus tells us that a house divided against itself will surely fall (Mark 3:25). Our feet won't walk both in the world and with Christ. The paths are divergent. We are forced to pick one path over the other.

And this fork in the road—this moment when we realize we cannot live a divided life any longer—is a gift of mercy. It is a tool in the tender hands of our loving God to woo us to himself. In that moment when we are gasping for breath on the floor, he is saying, "Come to me . . . and you will find rest for your souls" (Matt. 11:28–29).

## That Moment

We all have that moment when we come to the end of ourselves. For Christians, it should lead us to Christ. Without that moment, we continue in our own strength, pursuing our own goals, behaving as if we belong to ourselves. It's grace to us that our roots wither in untrue soil. The crisis of unhappiness that so many women are currently enduring, described in chapter 1, is a gift of God. It's the light on the dashboard warning us that something is wrong. It's the fading grass that tells the gardener the soil is no good.

In that moment, when we're at the end of our ropes, many dig in and insist that our way is the right way. We redouble our efforts, reaffirm our self-focused path, and determine to have the double life—our goals and dreams *plus* a little bit of Jesus when needed.

Author Gloria Furman says, "The bootstraps of self-righteousness are chains."[3] We try and try to pull ourselves up, but rather than being liberated, we are enslaved. We try harder, run faster, and spin our wheels in an exhausting attempt to create our own righteousness—the life, the freedom, the joy we've always wanted.

Rather than finding freedom, we dig ourselves into holes, as C. S. Lewis wrote. He said we behave as if we belong to ourselves, and this leads us down the wrong track, puts us on the ground floor, and brings us to a point of wanting to start over, to get out of our holes.[4]

## God Gives Us More Than We Can Handle

Undoubtedly you've heard the comforting American quip, *God never gives us more than we can handle*. And perhaps you've thought to yourself, *Really? Because this feels like a lot more than I can handle*. I'm with you—in my experience, God often gives us way more than we're comfortable with, so that we might cry out to him. These crises, these crossroads, are a call "that [we] should seek God, and perhaps feel [our] way toward him and find him. Yet he is actually not far from each one of us" (Acts 17:27).

This turning to God is a sort of death. We ultimately realize we cannot handle ourselves, our souls, our futures, our contentment. We need something, someone, outside of ourselves. We need our Creator who is also our Redeemer, our rescuer, our load bearer.

The moments we realize we need a Redeemer are as diverse as we are. For some it comes in a hospital bed or

3. Gloria Furman, *The Pastor's Wife: Strengthened by Grace for a Life of Love* (Wheaton, IL: Crossway, 2015), 31.
4. C. S. Lewis, *Mere Christianity* (New York: HarperCollins,1952), 16–17.

following a trauma. For others, God intervenes through friends or circumstances or even dreams. God may draw you in when you least expect it—when you've reached a goal and pinnacle in life and it doesn't taste as sweet as you thought it would. Even those who grew up in Christian homes must face moments when the Lord gives them more than they can handle.

We all find ourselves on the floor at one time or another—or even several times over. It might be the death of a loved one, an unforeseen broken marriage, a miscarriage, our own moral failure and shocking fall into temptation, or living far away from home and our usual coping methods. All of us must choose if we will cry out to God and find him or if we will rely on our own strength, our own wisdom, our own man-made support.

As Lewis said, we find ourselves in a hole that we've dug. All the people who have ever walked the earth have sought to handle their own lives, their own circumstances, their own futures their own way. But God, in his mercy, gives us more than we can handle, that we may cry out to him, seek him, and find him.

Will we lay down the very shovels that dug our holes? Will we surrender? Will we allow God to help us? Will we repent?

## Your Life Is Not Your Own

As I shared in the introduction to this book, the Lord gave me more than I could handle when I was in college. It was the first time, but certainly not the last, that I was unable to fix myself. Prior to that moment in my life, when things were rough, when circumstances had me down, I was able to bring myself out of it. I was accustomed to snapping out of a bad mood or bad season or a bad whatever. But not that time. The sadness that God gave me was beyond me.

In God's providence I grabbed the dusty paperback Bible that I had brought with me to college but never cracked open. It felt like in those pages the Lord wanted to offer me healing and wholeness and freedom. But I also sensed in my heart that he wanted all of me—not just Sunday morning Jen, not just used-to-sometimes-go-to-youth-group Jen, not just moral-when-it's-convenient Jen.

As I emerged from that season of sadness, some of the apostle Paul's words written to the church at Corinth stuck with me. He said, "Do you not know that your body is a temple of the Holy Spirit within you, whom you have from God? You are not your own, for you were bought with a price. So glorify God in your body" (1 Cor. 6:19–20).

"You are not your own" struck me immediately. I was startled awake to the truth that because I was created by God, he had a say in my college major, my social life, who I dated, how I spent my money, and the career I would seek. Going to parties and drinking alcohol underage suddenly felt very wrong. Pursuing a career purely based off of the income I could hope to make rang hollow. Christ in me caused the pursuit of worldly accolades and the attention of people, for which I had been so hungry, to leave a bad taste in my mouth.

These words to the Corinthians have become a life verse for me. I am not my own. I was created and redeemed by someone else. It's his breath in my lungs. This first more-than-I-can-handle season, this crisis that put me on the floor, was when Jesus graciously rooted me in himself.

## What Is the Gospel?

If you've ever been to church, you've likely heard the word *gospel*. Maybe you've heard of the Gospel of Matthew, or the Gospel according to Mark, or Luke's Gospel, or John's. We call those first four books of the New Testament the Gospels. *Gospel* simply means good news. The first four books of the New Testament record the good news of Jesus's life, death, and resurrection. They are the personal accounts of Matthew, Mark, Luke, and John as they witnessed—or interviewed eyewitnesses about—the life of Jesus.

The word *gospel* can also be used to describe the good news shared in the Bible. To appreciate the good news, though, we must first understand the bad news. In the previous chapter, we explored what it means to be created by God for his glory. But all of us have turned from God and pursued our own glory. No one treasures the Lord according to his value and worth. Because we have turned away from our holy and just God, we deserve eternal punishment. The Bible is clear that all have sinned against God and all are destined for torment in hell (see Rom. 3:23; 6:23; John 3:36; 1 John 5:12).

But God, being rich in mercy, has made a way for us to escape hell. Jesus, who is God, willingly descended to earth and lived a perfect, sinless life. He then willingly died on a cross, bearing the punishment of our sins, and rose from the dead, conquering both sin and death, so that we who trust Christ as Savior might escape hell and instead reign with Jesus in heaven (see Eph. 2:1–10).

The good news does not end with our salvation and justification—or the reality that Jesus took our punishment while giving us his righteousness—but continues as the Holy Spirit takes up residence in us and helps us to treasure Christ more than ourselves. As we are sanctified, or changed from within to look more and more like our Savior, we grow increasingly satisfied and overjoyed in him. The good news culminates with heaven and earth being reconciled and restored by Christ. We who trust and treasure him will reign with him forever and ever (see 2 Tim. 2:11–13).

In an article titled "What Is the Christian Gospel?" pastor and author John Piper says,

> To believe the gospel is not only to accept the awesome truths that (1) God is holy, (2) we are hopeless sinners, (3) Christ died and rose again for sinners, and (4) this great salvation is enjoyed by faith in Christ—but believing the gospel is also to treasure Jesus Christ as your unsearchable riches. What makes the gospel Gospel is that it brings a person into the everlasting and ever-increasing joy of Jesus Christ.[5]

To believe the gospel and to trust Jesus as Savior is not only to escape damnation. It is also to be awakened to the freedom and joy available only in Christ. When we believe the gospel, it changes everything. Our understanding of our past, present, and future is reoriented from a self-focused way of life to a Jesus-focused way of life.

## What Does It Mean to Be Rooted in the Gospel?

To be rooted in the gospel is to be like the banyan trees of the tropics. The trees' roots are many. They shoot out from

---

5. John Piper, "What Is the Christian Gospel?," Desiring God website, June 5, 2002, https://www.desiringgod.org/articles/what-is-the-christian-gospel.

all over and reach down toward the nutrient-rich soil. The trees thrive because of their many roots and the luscious soil. The soil is just right—*exactly* what these organisms need. The nutrition causes the trees to grow tall and broad and to reproduce. The far-reaching roots enable the trees to stand firm in the midst of hurricane-force winds, which lash the tropics every year. Even the fiercest storms cannot uproot the banyans.

The banyan trees' roots connect the trees to their life source, the soil. We too must be rooted in our life source, which is the gospel. As Christians, we know that the gospel is the good news of salvation. It is our rescue from hell and deliverance to heaven.

But the gospel is also the truth that propels us and compels us in all things. It is the very foundation of our lives and worldview and understanding of reality. The gospel is the most basic and important truth for all people. Sending our roots into any other soil causes us to wither.

John Calvin writes, "For true doctrine is not a matter of the tongue, but of life: neither is the Christian doctrine grasped only by the intellect and memory, as truth is grasped in other fields of study. Rather, *doctrine is rightly received when it takes possession of the entire soul* and finds a dwelling place and shelter in the most intimate affections of the heart."[6]

In other words, to believe the truth about the gospel, one must do more than mentally assent to it. The truth of the gospel is meant to transform us. And if it does not, then we do not really believe. The gospel has something to say about how we spend our time, where we spend our money,

6. Calvin, *Little Book on the Christian Life*, 12–13. Emphasis added.

the goals we pursue, the careers we seek, the hobbies we enjoy, the food we eat—everything.

The gospel says that we are not our own.

## Paul Prayed That the Church Would Be Rooted

The word *rooted* appears in two places in the Bible. Both are found in letters written by Paul to two different church communities, which he helped to establish. One is to the church at Ephesus and one is to the church at Colossae. In both contexts, Paul urges his readers to be rooted in the gospel.

First, in his letter to the Ephesians, Paul says,

> For this reason I bow my knees before the Father, from whom every family in heaven and on earth is named, that according to the riches of his glory he may grant you to be strengthened with power through his Spirit in your inner being, so that Christ may dwell in your hearts through faith—*that you, being rooted and grounded in love*, may have strength to comprehend with all the saints what is the breadth and length and height and depth, and to *know the love of Christ* that surpasses knowledge, that *you may be filled with all the fullness of God*. (Eph. 3:14–19)

You can hear Paul's labor and love for the Ephesians in these words. First, he says he earnestly prays for them. He prays to the Father of every family, meaning we are all created by God. Paul says that he asks God to fill them with power from the Holy Spirit, so that Christ may dwell in them. He wants them to be rooted and grounded in love—not just any love, but the love of the Father, who gives us his Son and empowers us by the Spirit—which is the gospel.

The love of Christ that surpasses knowledge is communicated radically in the gospel message, which the Ephesians believed by faith and Paul longed for them to comprehend. He desired that they (and you and I!) be filled with the fullness of God. The gospel is not peripheral. It is not secondary. It is meant to be the very center of our lives as followers of Christ.

Paul closes his prayer with these powerful words: "Now to him who is able to do far more abundantly than all that we ask or think, according to the power at work within us, to him be glory in the church and in Christ Jesus throughout all generations, forever and ever. Amen" (Eph. 3:20–21).

When we believe the gospel by faith, when we are empowered by the Holy Spirit, when Christ dwells in our hearts, when we are filled with the fullness of God, then God is able to do far more abundantly than all we could ever ask or imagine! This is the power of the gospel in us. And when this power is at work, it brings glory to Jesus throughout all generations.

We will revisit this in chapter 6 when we look at what it means to be established in the gospel. When we are rooted in Christ and built up in Christ, we will be established in Christ. This leads to rest in the gospel—a rest that can do far more than we ever ask or imagine.

Second, in his letter to the Colossians, Paul says, "Therefore, *as you received Christ Jesus the Lord, so walk in him, rooted and built up in him and established in the faith,* just as you were taught, abounding in thanksgiving" (Col. 2:6–7).

This prayer points to that moment when the Colossians surrendered to the Lord and believed the gospel by grace, through faith. Paul says if you have received Christ, then be rooted in Christ, be built up in him, be established in him and grow from that foundation.

Receiving Christ, being rooted in the gospel, is a watershed moment. It changes everything. It takes possession of all who believe.

## Roots in the Gospel, Not in This World

Interestingly, Paul continues from this urging of the Colossians to be rooted in Christ with this exhortation: "See to it that no one takes you captive by philosophy and empty deceit, according to human tradition, according to the elemental spirits of the world, and not according to Christ" (Col. 2:8).

The age of self says that life and meaning begin and end with us. But this is empty deceit and a human-centered tradition.

Like the Colossians, we must be aware of the philosophy of our culture and measure it against the truth of the gospel. The cultural air we breathe says to believe in yourself and you will be saved. But the true gospel says, "Believe in the Lord Jesus, and you will be saved" (Acts 16:31).

The gospel truth that God is both our Creator and Redeemer is the only soil that will nourish us. When we come to the end of ourselves, we must examine the soil in which our hearts have taken root. Are we rooted in ourselves and this world, or in the power of him who made us and longs to save us? Does the one true God nourish our souls? Does he equip us for life and enable us to bring him glory? Or is our soil toxic?

Only God can make us aware of what is toxic in our soil. Only he can show us that we must seek sustenance that comes from him alone. When we are rooted in him, rooted in the gospel, our whole being is forever changed.

Several years ago while sitting at an outdoor lunch table in southeast Asia with a group of women, I watched my friend Shannon awaken to the gospel. We ladies were helping lead a camp at the orphanage where my daughter used to live. In preparation for the trip we had studied the book of James. Our lunchtime conversation turned toward James's words, particularly where he says faith without works is dead (James 2:14–17).

James's point is that true faith will manifest itself in the actions of the believer. Those who have embraced the grace and mercy of Jesus will want to extend grace and mercy to others. True Christians will be compassionate and generous. The conversation evolved from good works offered to the needy to other areas of life. The ladies became animated as they discussed how true faith is evident in a believer's marriage or motherhood or career or relationships in her neighborhood.

Shannon sat quietly listening, her eyes darting from one woman to the other. Finally, she pushed back her plastic lawn chair and said, "I think I'm going to throw up." I followed her as she distanced herself from the table and put her face in her hands.

After a few minutes, she said, "I don't think I'm a Christian. I believe what the Bible says, but my faith doesn't affect the rest of my life. It doesn't affect the lives of anyone in my family. We think it's true, but it's never actually played a role in how we live. I can't believe I'm not a Christian. I always thought I was."

What a good and joyous moment. Shannon had come to the end of herself. She wanted to know what steps she should take next. I encouraged her to simply pray—to tell her author and Redeemer that she was grateful for his gift of salvation and wanted to receive it and walk with him for the rest of her days. Right then and there, in the heat and the dust and with the rest of the ladies looking on, we locked arms, bowed heads, and she prayed.

It was in that moment that the gospel took possession of Shannon's soul. On that sacred ground the Holy Spirit moved in, gave her new life, eternity with him, and deep and lasting joy. She became rooted in Christ.

And so it is with all who believe: "If you confess with your mouth that Jesus is Lord and believe in your heart that God raised him from the dead, you will be saved. For with the heart one believes and is justified, and with the mouth one confesses and is saved" (Rom. 10:9–10).

This gospel rooting is just the beginning of a lifelong journey that we will continue to explore in the remainder of this book. Being rooted in the gospel is not the only step toward finding the lasting joy you're looking for, but it is the crucial first step.

## Questions for Personal or Group Reflection

1. Have you experienced "that moment"? What is your personal story in coming to the end of yourself and surrendering to Jesus?

2. When has God given you more than you can handle?

3. In the above section "What Is the Gospel?" which verses stir your heart?

4. Paul said to the Colossians, "As you received Christ Jesus the Lord, so walk in him, rooted and built up in him and established in the faith" (Col. 2:6–7). How might that look in your life right now? In what areas do you need to root in Christ Jesus?

5. Are you currently struggling with a divided life? How can your sisters in Christ help you, hold you accountable, and pray for you?

6. Respond to the quote "Doctrine is rightly received when it takes possession of the entire soul and finds a dwelling place and shelter in the most intimate affections of the heart." In what areas of your heart do you need to allow doctrine to take possession?

7. Read and mediate on Ephesians 3:14–21. Pray those verses for yourself.

# 4

# You Are What You Eat

One of my dearest friends is an identical twin. Though we've known each other for almost twenty years, I had never met Alivia's twin until a couple years ago. I had seen pictures of Alison, heard stories about her, and even spoken with her on the phone. Alison and Alivia's photos and voices seemed identical to me.

When Alison visited our church along with Alivia's family, they all thought it would be great fun to play a joke on me. You can see where this is going. In walked "Alivia" with all four of her children. She came right up to me, arms spread wide to hug me, as she always does. I knew immediately that something was amiss. Before she could embrace me, I thrust my arms forward and said, "Wait, wait, wait. What's going on?" We all erupted into laughter as Alivia peeked from around the corner, and I realized what they were up to. All the children were sorely disappointed that I hadn't fallen for the trick.

My husband, on the other hand, did not know what hit him. Mark was preparing for the church service when Alison, not playing a trick at all, approached him and extended her hand, "Mark, I just wanted to introduce myself." He wondered if Alivia had lost her mind. Apparently, Alison just kept chatting away while my husband stood there dumbfounded.

When my daughters saw Alison with all of Alivia's children toddling behind her, they assumed of course that she was Alivia. My youngest said she could not tell who was who at all. My older girls said they had a suspicion that Alison wasn't Alivia when she started to speak.

We all had different reactions to Alivia's twin based on how well we knew Alivia. I could see in Alison's eyes that this was not my friend. Though her hair, her mannerisms, her outfit, and even the way she walked were just like Alivia, I knew that was not her. And although Alivia had been in our home for years with all of us there, my children and husband had not sat with her, laughed with her, and cried with her, like I had.

Often, we can recognize a counterfeit only when we know the original very well. If we are not intimately acquainted with the real deal, we will not be able to spot a fake when it walks right in and shakes our hand. And so it is with spiritual truth. If you and I aren't intimately acquainted with how God has revealed himself and the truth through his Word, we are at risk for believing falsifications when they are presented to us as truth.

As we saw in chapter 1, the rise of the autonomous self has conquered all of our cultural frontiers. We've deified ourselves, and everything else in our culture must bow down. The church has not been unscathed by this revolution. Counterfeits have entered the church in sheep's clothing and caught us unawares.

We've slid from a God-centered faith to a me-centered faith without realizing it. Somewhere along the way, instead of asking *How can I serve God?* we began asking *How can God serve me?*

## A Me-Centered Relationship with Jesus

While this slide from God-centeredness to me-centeredness is largely due to the Siren call of self, it has also been inadvertently reinforced by the church's well-intentioned prioritization for believers to have a personal relationship with Jesus.

Indeed, personally surrendering to the Lord is crucial, as we saw in chapter 3. "That moment" must come for every Christian. Each individual must be rooted in Christ and abide in Christ. But like an oil spill on the ocean, that emphasis on a *personal* relationship has covered areas it was never meant to touch.

For example, the right encouragement and conviction for believers to have a personal quiet time with the Lord has been altered such that "we now believe the Bible addresses us immediately. This is clearly seen in the demand for Bible devotionals that morph Bible verses into God's private encouraging words just for me."[1] In other words, we no longer strive to study the Bible for what it is: the word of God. We instead look for special words meant just for personal application.

---

1. Glenn Paauw, *Saving the Bible from Ourselves: Learning to Read and Live the Bible Well* (Downer's Grove, IL: InterVarsity Press, 2016), chap. 12, Kindle edition.

I can relate to that. How many mornings have I sleepily turned in the Bible and asked God for a spiritual pick-me-up? Or how many times have I flipped the pages until I found the perfect line, the just-so encouragement for my situation? It's not that this approach is totally wrong, but it's not enough. It's far too focused on us and not the author.

The superficial use of the Scriptures in pursuit of what they can offer you and me individually is destructive because we don't know what we're missing. As we snack on little tidbits here and there, we miss the feast that God intended to serve us. In his book, *Saving the Bible from Ourselves*, Glenn Paauw says our "focus is personal benefit-centered rather than doctrinal system-centered. . . . It is doubtful, however, that when God gave us the Bible his intention was for us to cut and paste sacred souvenirs from it while leaving the story itself far behind."[2]

Theologian N. T. Wright calls this the "magic book" syndrome, "whose 'meaning' has little to do with what the first century authors intended."[3] Rather, Wright says we interpret Scripture according to our own particular sort of spirituality or lifestyle. I'm afraid we are guilty as charged. We insist on the Bible only serving our particular moment, our day, our needs, our habits, and we therefore miss out on a fuller, deeper understanding of God's big story.

We see this prioritization of self on the shelves of Christian bookstores. Christian discipleship has largely morphed into self-help. Books are written and marketed to help you

---

2. Paauw, *Saving the Bible from Ourselves*, chap. 7, Kindle edition.
3. N. T. Wright, *The New Testament and the People of God* (Minneapolis, MN: Augsburg Fortress, 1992), 4, as quoted in Paauw, *Saving the Bible from Ourselves*, chap. 5, Kindle edition.

make a better you. Rather than laying out the goodness of God, titles invite you to be your best self and to live your best life.

Self-focus is apparent in popular Christian music as well. If you spend an hour listening to the top-rated Christian songs on the radio, you will notice that many of the titles and lyrics are self-focused rather than God-focused. What's troublesome about worship music prioritizing self is that, as worship leader Keith Getty says, "What we sing becomes the grammar of what we believe."[4] Music is not neutral— it affects our minds, hearts, and souls. Me-centered songs reinforce our natural me-centered flesh and our me-centered culture.

In sum, whether it's in our quiet times, in our books, or in our music, we Christians are largely engaging a truncated gospel. Rather than seeking the Lord's leadership, we're seeking to lead him. Rather than submitting to almighty God, we're asking him to submit to us.

We're attempting to create God in our image, rather than walking as creatures made in his. Instead of asking *How can I serve God?* we are asking *How can God serve me?*

### Big Macs vs. Filet Mignons

It's like we're all eating a daily diet of Big Macs, when filet mignons are available. Junk food is edible. You can survive on it. For a while. A steady diet of Big Macs won't necessarily kill you. But too many days in a row of fast food is likely to leave you feeling sick and undernourished.

4. Joan Huyser-Honig, "Keith Getty on Writing Hymns for the Church Universal," Calvin Institute of Christian Worship, September 1, 2006, https://worship.calvin.edu/resources/resource-library/keith-getty-on-writing-hymns-for-the-church-universal/.

Not only that, but recent medical research shows that fast food is often addictive. Researchers and doctors now claim that ingredients in fast food alter the chemicals in our brains so that we want more.[5] Many of us can testify to getting stuck in a cycle of eating poorly and irrationally craving more of the junk.

But in our right minds—when we're rational and reasonable and take the time needed to make a measured decision rather than a rash one ruled by hunger pangs—who would choose a Big Mac if a juicy, tender, lean filet mignon was also available for the same price and at the same place? We'd probably all pick the steak. Why would we feast on junk food when healthy, whole, nourishing food is also on the table?

We're a generation that has been raised on spiritual fast food, and we're sick. It's time for us to sit down at the table, linger, and sup on the feast the King has for us. The gospel is the most nourishing food we could ingest for our souls. And it is devoid of self. It's all about Christ crucified, risen, and coming again.

To better understand the bad food we need to cut, let's look at the fast-food meals we've been dining on for the last few decades. We'll examine what it is about this food that's so unhealthy. And then we'll take a look at the filet mignon alternative. Hopefully, with God's help, by the end of this chapter you and I will be motivated to clean out our spiritual food pantries and recommit to a solid eating plan.

---

5. Mae Rice, "A New Study Shows the Scary Similarities between Junk Food and Drugs," Curiosity.com, August 17, 2018, https://curiosity.com/topics/a-new-study-shows-the-scary-similarities-between-junk-food-and-drugs-curiosity/.

## The Believe-in-Yourself Gospel

Me-centered teaching has crept in, set up camp, and been so widely accepted that we don't even wrestle with it anymore. *Believe-in-yourselfism* is the junk food I see doing the most damage today, for two reasons. First, it's attractive. We are naturally drawn to ourselves. Second, it is subtle and sneaky. DIY (Do-It-Yourself) is the rage in all areas: DIY home renovations, DIY online degrees, DIY marriage ceremonies, DIY orthodontics, DIY diagnosis and prescriptions. Why not DIY spirituality too?

The "believe-in-yourself gospel" is wreaking havoc on the church, especially in women's ministries. This false gospel says God wants you to be happy, you are enough just the way you are, and it's up to you to reach within to make yourself successful and satisfied.

This false gospel is the drumbeat of today's young women, professionals, working moms, stay-at-home moms, and mompreneuers. It's a nice pep talk we give to ourselves and to one another to conquer another day of college, singleness, motherhood, or work life. "Just believe in yourself," we rehearse. We've even got it painted on throw pillows, coffee mugs, and cute T-shirts. It's written on chalkboards, in blogs, and on Instagram feeds. It's everywhere.

Believe-in-yourselfism was born out of two other false gospels that have infiltrated the church in recent decades. These two extra value meals have melded together, making a powerful combo meal that's hard to resist.

The first is Moralistic Therapeutic Deism (MTD), which was first coined in 2005 when sociologists Christian Smith and Melinda Lundquist Denton interviewed about three thousand teenagers and recorded their findings in their book *Soul Searching: The Religious and Spiritual Lives of American Teenagers.*[6]

MTD can be summed up like this: there is a god, and he wants us to be happy ourselves and nice to others. He's needed only when one of those values is threatened. And all good people go to heaven when they die. I must agree with the researchers who conclude that "a significant part of Christianity in the United States is actually [only] tenuously Christian in any sense that is seriously connected to the actual historical Christian tradition, but is rather substantially morphed into Christianity's misbegotten step-cousin, Christian Moralistic Therapeutic Deism."[7]

Not only are individual Christians ingesting a diet of MTD, but institutional Christendom in America is eating it up, as well. Al Mohler comments on the study: "This distortion of Christianity has taken root not only in the minds of individuals, but also 'within the structures of at least some Christian organizations and institutions.'"[8]

This means that our churches, as well as our Christian schools, colleges, community Bible studies, and neighborhood ministries are reinforcing the false messages of MTD. In multiple contexts, Christians are hearing that God wants you to be happy and nice, he'll stay out of the way unless you need to call on him for either of those goals, and as long as you're a good person, you'll go to heaven when you die.

---

6. Christian Smith and Melina Lundquist Denton, *Soul Searching: The Religious and Spiritual Lives of American Teenagers* (New York: Oxford University Press, 2005).

7. Smith and Denton, as quoted in Albert Mohler, "Moralistic Therapeutic Deism—the New American Religion," April 11, 2005, Albert Mohler website, https://albertmohler.com/2005/04/11/moralistic-therapeutic-deism-the-new -american-religion-2/.

8. Mohler, "Moralistic Therapeutic Deism."

Does this sound like a meal you've eaten lately? Or one that your church or the book on your nightstand is serving up?

A second contributor to believe-in-yourselfism is the health and wealth gospel. In its most basic form, this false gospel says that you and I can be healthy and wealthy if only we have enough faith. You might be picturing the over-the-top television preachers who have clearly strayed from biblical teaching. But the health and wealth gospel is actually subtle and sinister.

It surfaces in an unspoken but widely held belief that God wants me to be happy and successful. As his child, I should not expect suffering or difficulties in this life.

But this false teaching is contrary to Scripture. Jesus said, "If anyone would come after me, let him deny himself and take up his cross and follow me. For whoever would save his life will lose it, but whoever loses his life for my sake will find it. For what will it profit a man if he gains the whole world and forfeits his soul?" (Matt. 16:24–26).

In spite of this clear teaching in Scripture, health and wealth teaching "can seem to be a necessary inference from some Christian texts and teachings and it can be absorbed from the attitudes of others in a community."[9] Whether we state it or not, many of us are subsisting on the health and wealth gospel and causing others to do the same in the practical outworking of our fast-food faith.

## Breaking Our Addiction to Happy Meals

Believe-in-yourselfism, the outgrowth of MTD and health and wealth, is the meal we're most likely to order today.

---

9. Timothy Keller, *Making Sense of God: Finding God in the Modern World* (New York: Penguin, 2016), 51.

It is dangerous because it sounds good and feels good and contains a morsel of truth. It is indeed biblical to say that you and I were created by a good God who made us in his good image and gave us good gifts, skills, and abilities to work hard to accomplish much while we're here.

But this thinking becomes immediately bankrupt when we rely on ourselves and turn inward for strength. It becomes a false gospel because it's an inward gospel. In fact, it's a form of legalism. We expect blessing based on our own self-driven efforts. We expect to earn our salvation by digging deep and trying harder. It says "do this" and you should "get that." It's a prescription to behave a certain way in order to attain certain results.

We see this kind of thinking distilled in the thesis of a recent and popular book. The author writes, "You, and only you, are ultimately responsible for who you become and how happy you are."[10] Rather than a focus on Christ, the focus is on self. When we succumb to this paradigm, we are required to be our own saviors.

My friend Steph recently put the shrapnel of this false teaching on display. Steph has two young sons and is in the midst of an exhausting season of life that I remember well. It's the season where a stretch of five hours of sleep feels like a winter's hibernation and a trip alone to Target feels like a day at the spa. Steph came to Bible study at my house weary and heavy-laden. She couldn't hold back the tears.

Reacting to text messages from her friends who believed that she needed to do more to make herself happy, Steph said, "It makes me feel terrible. It makes me feel like I have

10. Rachel Hollis, *Girl, Wash Your Face: Stop Believing the Lies About Who You Are So You Can Become Who You Were Meant to Be* (Nashville: Nelson Books, 2018), xi.

to make it all happen. I can't live up to what my girlfriends are telling me to do. I haven't even showered this week."

You and I and Steph will never be rescued by our good behavior. We'll never be able to author our own happiness. Lasting joy comes from Jesus, not from within. As author and pastor Jared Wilson says, "The essence of the Christian message is not 'Behave!' but 'Behold!'"[11]

The heart of spiritual junk food is that it tells us how to behave rather than calling us to behold. Behold who? Jesus. Any deviation from biblical Christianity can be detected when we are told to turn our practices and habits inward on ourselves, rather than outward on our marvelous Savior.

## Confession Leads to Joy

Spiritual junk food prioritizes happiness, but it's not a deep-down soul happiness. It's quick, cheap, and easy—just like its physical fast food counterpart. Our inner strength runs out, our happiness doesn't last, and we're hungry again in no time. We get addicted to the feel-good message and crave more. But each time we eat it, like a drug it doesn't go as far as it did the last time. We need higher doses at each meal to pump ourselves up and march on.

What you and I need more than temporary happiness is eternal joy. And confession is the gateway. *Confession leads to joy.*

When we confess that we are not enough; that we don't have the power within ourselves to be fulfilled; that we sin; that we fall short; that we make messes of our own lives and others'; that we cannot make it in this life on our

11. Jared C. Wilson (@jaredcwilson), Twitter, November 7, 2013, 12:41 p.m., https://twitter.com/jaredcwilson.

own; that Jesus is the only way, the only truth, and the only life, then we can finally unclench our white-knuckle grip and exhale.

Doesn't it feel good to let go? Your life is not your own. You are not enough. You are not all you need. But Jesus is there. And he *is* enough. He is your life. He is all you need. Breathe.

Our culture keeps drawing our eyes back to ourselves, but they belong on Jesus. We must acknowledge, confess, repent, and repeat. The habit and practice of confession and repentance "pushes back on secular liturgies of self-confidence that, all week long, are implicitly teaching you to 'believe in yourself'—false gospels of self-assertion that refuse grace."[12]

To believe in oneself is to refuse grace. It is to say to the God who made you, *I'm doing fine on my own, thank you very much.* It is to refuse the Lord's unconditional love, forgiveness, and empowerment. But when we confess that *we are not enough*, we invite all of that in. Confession leads to joy.

An initial coming to the end of ourselves, confession, and repentance leads us to "that moment" we looked at in chapter 3—when we become rooted in Christ. When we are initially saved by grace. But it's grace first and *still grace forever*. By grace we are saved and by grace we must walk. For God's power is made perfect in weakness (2 Cor. 12:9–10).

We not only enter our relationship with Christ by grace, but grace is also how our relationship is sustained. It's a routine cycle of coming to the end of ourselves and renewing our minds in what's true—confessing that we fall short and need him every hour.

---

12. James K. A. Smith, *You Are What You Love: The Spiritual Power of Habit* (Grand Rapids, MI: Brazos Press, 2016), 97.

We are tempted every hour to eat the junk food and not the filet mignon. We are easily tricked, too hungry to wait, willing to sell out for the fast food rather than the slow-cooked goodness.

As we are rooted in Christ, so we must build ourselves up, or nourish ourselves, in Christ.

## Make a Diet Change from Me-ology to Theology

Me-ology is the junk food diet we've been serving up in our spiritual lives. The healthy alternative we need to immediately start ingesting is theology.[13] Theology is the study of God. It is the examination of his attributes and abilities, his goodness and faithfulness, who he is and what he has done. Theology is substantial, true, and life-giving. Feasting here will allow us to grow stronger and more into the image of him who made us.

Me-ology is frail, precarious, and dependent on you and me who grow tired and weary and make mistakes. Me-ology is only as good as we are. And we never feel quite smart enough, or disciplined enough, or pretty enough, or energetic enough, or whatever enough.

We are finite. Jesus is infinite. We are limited, he is limitless. We are selfish, he is selfless. We need sleep, he never sleeps. We are weak, he is strong. Me-ology prizes you and me. Theology prizes the God of the universe who holds everything together.

When we center our lives and our spiritual diet on theology rather than on me-ology, we choose to renew our minds in the boundless worth of our Lord in heaven, rather than

13. For more on "me-ology," listen to Blair Linne's "Sacred Science," Philadelphia Lamp Mode Recordings, April 9, 2013.

in the very limited power of ourselves. We lift our eyes off of ourselves, off of the mirror, and off of our social media accounts, and we raise them high to the King who is wise and able and kind and trustworthy and true. In the next chapter we will study the practical ways we can do just that.

The irony is that when we make the change from me-ology to theology, our "sense of worth or value that comes through faith in Christ is arguably more secure."[14] Our intuition says the more we prioritize ourselves, the better we will feel about ourselves. But in reality, the more you and I look at ourselves, the more we loath ourselves because we fall short.

When we fix our eyes on Jesus, when we behold our good God and ponder what he has done, your self-worth and mine is elevated. We remember that we have inherent value as dearly created children. We remember that we are chosen, adopted, and loved (see Gal. 3:26–27).

In other words, when we transition from self-focus to Jesus-focus, we actually end up with a better self-image—because it's dependent on him who made us, not on ourselves.

Because God is the author of our lives and the Redeemer of our souls, we will thrive when we study him, know him, love him, root ourselves in him, and renew our minds in him. Feasting on him, beholding him, and making the change from me-ology to theology is the key to your well-being and mine.

C. S. Lewis put it this way: "The more we get what we now call 'ourselves' out of the way and let Him take us over, the more truly ourselves we become."[15]

---

14. Keller, *Making Sense of God*, 139.
15. C. S. Lewis, *Mere Christianity* (New York: HarperCollins, 1952), 225.

## Retraining Our Palates

The good news is that we can retrain our palates. We don't have to stay addicted to spiritual junk food. We can remove the junk and replace it with real sustenance.

You already know that when my girls were little, we lived in Japan. My kids went through the terrible twos and threes and the obstinate fours and the sassy fives while we were subsisting on an Asian diet, with all of its interesting tastes and smells.

My husband and I decided at the outset that we would insist that our girls eat whatever food was served to them. That's part of the missionary or pastor's kid gig. You get invited to many places, and there's usually food. We didn't want our kids to refuse food given to them, so we practiced at every meal.

If they did not want to eat something that we served them at home, we did not make them sit at the table until it was gone. I simply wrapped it up and said, "You don't have to eat it now, but this will be the very next thing you eat. You cannot eat the next snack or meal served until this is gone." It worked. They eventually got hungry enough that they ate whatever had previously been an aversion. Yes, sometimes they ate brussels sprouts for breakfast. But praise God, other than a unanimous and perplexing aversion to tomatoes, they're not particularly picky eaters.

Physical palates can be trained and retrained. And so can spiritual palates. It is possible for you and me to begin to identify the spiritual junk food we've been ingesting and instead make healthy choices that will fuel our spiritual growth. We can clear the junk off the table and out of the kitchen and start making better choices today.

As with any addiction or bad habit, it will not be easy in the beginning—we will initially crave the quick and cheap choices we're used to. But as our good choices begin to stack up, we'll start to feel a nourishing change from the inside out. Our taste buds will mature. We'll notice good ingredients and bad ingredients more quickly. Discernment will lead to nourishment, and you and I will thrive the way we were made to.

## Turning from Self

The believe-in-yourself gospel is attractive at first. "You got this, girlfriend," makes a fun T-shirt. But when we root ourselves in Christ Jesus, we must also decide to continually build ourselves up in Christ Jesus, as Colossians 2:6–7 says. The self-help gospel is indeed a Siren song, and I am lured back to it on a daily basis. How quickly I forget that it's God who is the source of my life, not me! And how quickly I am reminded that I need him when I get to the end of myself.

You and I must repeatedly confess our need for Jesus. We must confess our bankruptcy and his wealth. We must remember and say out loud for him and ourselves to hear that we bring nothing to the table. He alone is the one who holds everything together.

There is one true Jesus, and he has made himself known to us. Let's get to know the true gospel of Jesus so well that we can spot a counterfeit gospel when it looms on the horizon, walks into our churches, or pops up in our women's Bible studies.

## Questions for Personal or Group Reflection

1. Have you witnessed Christian culture in North America increasingly ask *How can God serve me?* rather than *How can*

*I serve God*? Do you personally feel a temptation toward that perspective?

2. What is good and right about focusing on a personal relationship with Jesus? How can that be prioritized to a fault?

3. Do you ever suffer from the "magic book syndrome," treating the Bible as if it has a special word just for you today? How is that a limited, at best, and destructive, at worst, practice?

4. Does believe-in-yourselfism show up in your community of faith, books, or worship songs? Have you experienced the inadequacy of believing in yourself?

5. Can you identify some junk food that you need to throw out?

6. Read and discuss or meditate on Psalm 36. Write down the strong words used to describe God and his ways.

7. Read 2 Corinthians 12:7–10 and identify some of the weaknesses God has given you. In what ways can you be thankful for them? In what ways has God proven strong and faithful in them?

# Built Up in Christ

When I was in sixth grade, I met Jordan Knight. Backstage at the New Kids on the Block concert, he asked me if I thought he should shave before going on stage. Are you dying? I died.

My friend got us backstage passes, and we met both Jordan Knight and Donnie Wahlberg. For eleven-year-old Jen (Jenni at the time), it was euphoric. I mean, I actually touched Jordan's face.

My bedroom walls were plastered with NKOTB posters. I had NKOTB bed sheets. Cassette tapes. A beach towel. A lunch box. I even had a black felt fedora just like the New Kids, and I proudly wore it to the mall.

Maybe you had the same experience with the Backstreet Boys or *NSYNC or Boyz II Men. My oldest daughter had a thing for One Direction. What is it with boy bands? They have a special power over the preteen girl. We were smitten. Obsessed even.

No one had to convince us to love them. We didn't need to be told their many virtues or attend a class to learn all their excellencies. Like moths to a flame, we swarmed without instruction. It was natural and automatic.

I may be thirty years past my backstage moment with Jordan Knight, but I am still drawn to the things I adore. Some of those things are superficial, like the black iron chandelier I'd like to have for my dining room. Or this season's new line of athleisure wear. Or a new leather handbag. Some of the things I adore are a bit more meaningful, like the books on my Amazon wish list and a desire for a healthy lifestyle. Other objects of my affection are truly important, like the vision I have of a peaceful home, game nights with my kids, ministry side by side with my husband, deep spiritual conversations with the women in my life, restful vacations with my loved ones, and the perfect work-life balance.

We all naturally adore something or many somethings. You and I and everyone else on the planet have an idea of what we want. Author James K. A. Smith says, "To be human is to be animated and oriented by some vision of 'the good life.' . . . To be human, is to be a lover and to love something ultimate."[1] He says the heart is like a compass. It automatically points us toward our true north—that is, whatever we want or love or envision as the good life. Like a magnet, the object of our affection pulls us toward itself. We don't have to be taught to go there; we naturally wander that way.

## What Do You Want?

In the very beginning of his ministry, Jesus turned to his disciples, who had just started following him, and asked

1. James K. A. Smith, *You Are What You Love: The Spiritual Power of Habit* (Grand Rapids, MI: Brazos Press, 2016), 12–13, 15.

them, "What do you want?" (John 1:38 NIV). Some translations say "What are you seeking?" or "What are you looking for?"

Jesus asked this question during their first moments together because he knew they were all inclined to follow whatever it was they wanted or loved. He wanted them to identify what it was they were after. He knew that the heart is the wellspring of life (Prov. 4:23). It is out of the abundance of the heart that we live (Luke 6:45).

Life is lived in minutes, which add up to hours and days and years. Whatever we love most each minute is what drives our action in the present. Those minutes build, one on top of the other. Life is a culmination of our momentary desires. Whatever our hearts love each minute will lead us for a lifetime. We are what we love.

Each of us must therefore ask, What do I love? What am I loving the most right now? Jesus calls us to love God and to love neighbor above all else (Matt. 22:36–40), so we run into problems when we love other things more than these. The problem isn't necessarily that we love certain things; it's that often we don't love the right things enough.

For example, if I love myself and my schedule and my convenience more than I love my neighbor, then I won't be willing to offer help when needed. I'll be unable, for example, to watch a friend's child while she goes to the doctor; reserve a spot on our family's calendar to serve at our local food bank once a month; or joyfully spend one morning a week with my ailing father in his nursing home.

Or if I love myself more than I love the Lord, I'll spend more time perfecting my own image, my own home, and my own work than I will getting to know him better through prayer, time in the word, and worship.

The problem isn't that I love to have a schedule or work hard or have a nice house or even necessarily that I love myself. The problem is that I don't love either God or my neighbor enough. And my loves are out of order.

## Cultural Magnets

The objects of our love are more caught than taught. No one has to teach me to desire a better chandelier in my dining room. I want a new light because I see prettier lights in other people's homes, on the covers of home design magazines in the grocery store, and when I tune in to HGTV. The prettier lights are all around me, and they make my current light look ugly. I am immersed in a culture of pretty home things. I see them. I talk about them with my friends. I want them.

Amazon and Google know this well. Recently I was at a friend's home for our Gospel Community (our church's version of small group or community group). The cell reception in her area was bad so I logged on to her Wi-Fi on my phone. The next day my Facebook feed was filled with advertisements for the exact rug in my friend's living room. Not only her rug, but her lamp and chair as well. The internet knew where I had been; and it knew that I would see that rug there because it had been ordered from her IP address. It knew that I would like what I saw, and it gave me a chance to purchase it the very next day.

Amazon and Google and Facebook know that we humans are shortsighted. We see and live for and love the here and now. It's hard for us to envision a good life that is outside of our immediate surroundings. Smith says, "We might not realize the ways we're being covertly trained to hunger and thirst for idols that can never satisfy."[2]

So if our hearts are like a compass and they naturally align with whatever we love, then the work of the Christian is to constantly turn our compasses back to our true north—to God himself, the only one who can truly satisfy you and me.

## Prone to Wander, So We Must Renew

By the time my family moved away from Japan, I had spent more time in my life driving on the left side of the road than on the right side. When we relocated to right-side-of-the-road countries, I often approached my car and got in on the right side instead of the left. I ended up in the passenger seat when I was supposed to be the driver more times than I care to admit. If I was alone, I had a good laugh. If I was with my kids, they definitely had a good laugh.

I was prone to getting into the right side of the car because that's what I was used to. It was my intuition. It was natural. But it was wrong. I had to retrain myself to get into the left side of the car when I was going to drive it. In the same way, we are prone to loving ourselves and other things more than we love God. Therefore we have to constantly retrain ourselves.

The Bible calls this renewing your mind. The apostle Paul knew how easily we are influenced by the cultural love-magnets all around us. He knew the cultural air we breathe would not point us back to our supreme love,

---

2. Smith, *You Are What You Love*, 59.

which is God himself. So he instructed the early church to renew their minds.

In his letter to the Romans Paul said, "Do not be conformed to this world, but be transformed by the renewal of your mind" (Rom. 12:2). He told the Ephesians to "be renewed in the spirit of your minds" (Eph. 4:23). To renew your mind is to be built up in Christ (Col. 2:7).

Unworthy objects will constantly pull the compass of our hearts toward them, so renew—remember what is true. Remember who is the source of your life and breath. Remember your Creator and sustainer and the giver of your true joy.

Renew your mind. Remind yourself. Rehearse the truth to one another. Just as you were rooted in Christ, so build yourselves up in Christ.

In renewing their minds Paul wanted the early Christians to set their minds on the things above. Rather than simply behave, he wanted them to behold their God. He told the Colossians, "If then you have been raised with Christ, seek the things that are above, where Christ is, seated at the right hand of God. Set your minds on things that are above, not on things that are on earth" (Col. 3:1–2).

In other words, Paul says we must take our eyes and hearts off of what we see and look up. He wants us to stop navel-gazing and behold our God. We calibrate our hearts to our supreme love by looking up at him, not out at the temporal landscape before us. We must be intentional about where our hearts and minds wander, because a wandering heart has disordered loves. It naturally gravitates toward what is seen, what is instant, what is gratifying right now. To properly order our loves, we must fix our eyes on Jesus.

## Schedules, Budgets, and Such

Have you noticed that self-control begets self-control? And conversely, indulgence begets indulgence? I have seen this phenomenon play out in my own life.

When I stay within our family's monthly financial budget, then I am also more likely to stay on task within the boundaries of my calendar, stay committed to my exercise regimen, and eat according to a well-balanced diet. It seems that one area of self-control in my life leads to further self-control in the other areas. And when I go out-of-bounds in one place, I go out-of-bounds elsewhere.

Routines, schedules, and budgets are wise. We frown on them because we don't like to be constrained, but we know they're good for us. In fact, we know that they actually lead to greater freedom because we aren't bogged down by exhaustion, debt, and regret. King Solomon, who was given supernatural wisdom from God, said, "A man without self-control is like a city broken into and left without walls" (Prov. 25:28). The boundary of the wall gives the city's inhabitants freedom.

We know the good we ought to do, but we don't do it. We know it's better to stay within a budget, to stay on task, to eat healthy, to get exercise, and to sleep eight hours a night.

It's not a matter of *knowing* what's best; it's a matter of *loving* what's best.

As children of the Enlightenment we tend to think that the more we know, the better we will be. How often do we repeat clichés such as *knowledge is power*? This philosophy has also crept into the church. I agree with Smith who says, "We often approach discipleship as primarily a didactic endeavor—as if becoming a disciple of Jesus is largely an intellectual project, a matter of acquiring knowledge."[3]

Knowledge alone does not ensure mature Christian growth, for two reasons. The first is that we are driven by our love more than our knowledge. The second is that we need a power outside of us to help us. As C. S. Lewis said, "Even the best Christian that ever lived is not acting on his own steam."[4]

## Where Does Our Help Come From?

Our own steam runs out. We cannot rely on ourselves to make us love God more than anything or anyone else. We simply cannot *will* it to happen. We need a helper.

The psalmist wrote, "I lift up my eyes to the hills. / From where does my help come? / My help comes from the Lord, / who made heaven and earth" (Ps. 121:1–2). This particular psalm is included in a grouping of fifteen psalms of ascent, written for Israel to sing on the way up the Temple Mount in Jerusalem to worship God. The psalmist lifted his eyes and looked toward the temple, where God was especially present with his people. He acknowledged that he needed the Lord's help, even for his journey of worship. And so do you and I.

We looked closely in chapter 3 at the good news of the gospel—how we initially become rooted in Christ through our salvation. We acknowledged that the Spirit woos us— God the Father through his Son and by his Spirit draws us into a relationship with him. And it's all by grace. By grace you and I were saved, not from our own efforts, it is the gift of God (Eph. 2:8).

---

3. Smith, *You Are What You Love*, 3.
4. C. S. Lewis, *Mere Christianity* (New York: HarperCollins, 1952), 63.

Grace does not end with salvation. No, you and I need it also for our sanctification. To *sanctify* means to make holy or to purify from sin or to consecrate.[5] We use the term to refer to our growth in Christlikeness. It's the journey of spiritual maturity from salvation to the end of our days. What we often forget, though, is that not only is our salvation by grace, but our sanctification is as well.

We tend to be like the Galatian Christians. They were saved by grace through faith, but then they attempted to earn merit through doing works of the law. In other words, they wanted to sanctify themselves with their own acts, in their own efforts, for their own credit. Paul asked them, "Are you so foolish? Having begun by the Spirit, are you now being perfected by the flesh?" (Gal. 3:3).

He wanted to know why, if they had been saved by a wooing of the Spirit through grace, were they trying to mature through their own efforts? You can almost hear him saying, *You can't do that! It's not possible. It was the Spirit who saved you and it's the Spirit who will sanctify you. All is grace. You were saved by grace, and you'll grow by grace.*

We need to hear these words too. We are quick to return to ourselves, our own steam, our own efforts. But they run out. Like my getting into the wrong side of the car over and over, our intuition is to return to self-reliance and self-help. But if we are going to have any success in renewing our minds, we need the Spirit's help. We need to lift our eyes and remember that our help comes from the Lord.

Paul writes to the Colossians, "For this I toil, struggling with all [Christ's] energy that he powerfully works within me" (Col. 1:29). Paul exerted himself. He toiled. But he knew

5. Dictionary.com (2019), s.v. "sanctification," https://www.dictionary.com/browse/sanctification, accessed October 20, 2018.

it was God's energy that was powerfully working in him. He knew where his help came from.

As you and I seek to be built up in Christ, we too must remember that it's his energy that works in us. We must lift our eyes and remember our Helper. We cannot will our spiritual growth. We cannot will our love for God. We need his help in supplying it.

I have had seasons of faith that felt very dry. I've faced days and weeks when I didn't feel like praying at all. Reading the Bible felt like a chore, not a joy. Spiritual endeavors seemed like rote activities that were far from life-giving. I've faced days when I didn't want to acknowledge the Lord or engage with him at all.

On those days I find it helpful to pray, "Lord, help me to want you. Actually, Lord, I need to back up from there. Help me to even *want* to want you." Some valleys require that kind of prayer. And that's okay, because my salvation and my sanctification are both rooted in grace. They are both the work of the Spirit. It is good for me to lift my eyes and remember my help comes from the Lord, the Maker of heaven and earth.

## But We Do Toil

Paul was by no means passive when it came to his own spiritual growth and ministry in helping others grow. We see in his letter to the Colossians, that he *toiled*. He knew that all he did was a gift of grace from God. Foundational to his efforts was his understanding that the Spirit worked in him.

He fleshed this out when he wrote to the Corinthians: "But by the grace of God I am what I am, and his grace toward me was not in vain. On the contrary, I worked harder than any of them, though it was not I, but the grace of God that is with me" (1 Cor. 15:10).

He told his mentee Timothy to *train* himself for godliness (1 Tim. 4:7), and Paul prayed that the church at Ephesus would know "what is the immeasurable greatness of [God's] power toward us who believe, according to the working of his great might" (Eph. 1:19).

This raises the question: As women rooted in Christ who desire to renew our minds in Christ, how do we actually go about that? What are the practicalities of our training in godliness, which we acknowledge comes by the power of the Spirit alone?

## Be Renewed: Some Practices

In chapter 2 we explored what it means to be made in God's image. You and I bear God's character and goodness. But sin has marred his image in us. When we renew our minds, we rewind and remember who we are in Christ. As Smith writes, the goal of our sanctification is "a renewal of the mandate in creation: to be (re)made in God's image and then sent as his image bearers *to* and *for* the world."[6]

How then, by the Spirit's power, might we pursue being renewed or built up in Christ? The ideas below are not a how-to manual. They are not a list to obey in order to achieve certain results.

These activities are simply the conduits I have observed the Lord use to grow his followers in the two decades that I have been in ministry.

---

6. Smith, *You Are What You Love*, 88.

### Confession and Prayer

Of utmost importance in renewing our minds is a foundation of confession. As we saw in chapter 4, confession is the gateway to joy. We must come to our toil with an awareness that we are inadequate. A can-do attitude based in self-reliance will ring hollow, lead to burnout, and might even cause us to sense that God has betrayed us because he didn't deliver on our efforts. We must first and frequently confess that apart from God we can do nothing (John 15:5).

On the night before he went to the cross, Jesus comforted his disciples in the upper room saying, "I will ask the Father, and he will give you another Helper, to be with you forever. . . . He dwells with you and will be in you. . . . He will teach you all things and bring to your remembrance all that I have said to you" (John 14:16–17, 26). Jesus knew their need—*our* need—for help.

Prayer takes on many forms. You and I can breathe a quick prayer in the midst of a difficult moment and ask the Spirit to help us, just as we can offer a quick prayer of praise in the midst of joy. We can pray before we open the Bible and ask the Spirit to supernaturally illumine our minds. We can pray before meeting with friend, family, or foe, asking him to help us be a blessing and a light in that situation. We can pray for an extended period of time—a long quiet time in the morning where we bring everything to mind before the Lord, or a journaled prayer in the evening. We can and should fast and pray from time to time. Whatever and however we pray, prayer reminds us that we are weak but God is strong, and we need him every hour.

## The Word of God

On the floor of my dorm room, coming to the end of myself my freshman year in college, I reached for my dusty Bible, and it was nothing less than supernatural. God, in his mercy and kindness, had compassion on my broken heart and wooed me to himself. Because of the great love with which he loved me, he revealed himself to me in his word.

The author of the book of Hebrews said, "The word of God is living and active, sharper than any two-edged sword, piercing to the division of soul and of spirit, of joints and of marrow, and discerning the thoughts and intentions of the heart" (Heb. 4:12). The words of Jesus in the garden of Gethsemane pierced my soul and my heart. I read the story of the cross, was overwhelmed by Jesus's great love for me, and committed myself to his lordship for the rest of my days.

Paul told Timothy that "all Scripture is breathed out by God and profitable for teaching, for reproof, for correction, and for training in righteousness, that the man of God may be complete, equipped for every good work" (2 Tim. 3:16–17). If the Bible is anything, it is *able*. Because it is the living word of our living God, it is able to speak to every facet of your life and mine.

If we want to know who our God is—his character, his capabilities, his history, the promises he has kept in the past and the ones he's made for the future—we must turn to his word. We can know the Maker of heaven and earth because he has made himself known to us in the Bible.

In her important and practical book *Women of the Word*, Jen Wilkin says, "Bible literacy matters because it protects us from falling into error. Both the false teacher and the secular humanist rely on biblical ignorance for their messages to take root, and the modern church has proven fertile ground for those messages."[7] The best way for you and me to know God and to discern a counterfeit is to know God's word.

Just as one day a week at the gym won't make us physically fit, so sporadic time in the word of God won't make us spiritually fit. We won't really know what's in there or be changed by it unless we invest ourselves in it. Wilkin says, "Gaining Bible literacy requires allowing our study to have a cumulative effect—across weeks, months, years—so that the interrelation of one part of Scripture to another reveals itself slowly and gracefully, like a dust cloth slipping inch by inch from the face of a masterpiece."[8]

If you and I are going to trust the Lord, we need to know him well. And to do that, we must invest time reading, studying, memorizing, and applying his word. The Bible is not primarily for our information, but for our transformation. It is meant, as the book of Hebrews says, to pierce our soul and spirit, and to discern our thoughts and the intentions of our hearts.

If we pray and confess that we need the Spirit to help us, he will teach us all things (John 14:26) as we study his word. Not only that, but he will train us, make us complete, and equip us for every good work (2 Tim. 3:16–17). While studying the Bible alone is beneficial, studying it with the people of God is especially powerful.

---

7. Jen Wilkin, *Women of the Word: How to Study the Bible with Both Our Hearts and Our Minds* (Wheaton, IL: Crossway, 2014), 45.
8. Wilkin, *Women of the Word*, 75.

### The People of God

We were made for community. It's for our good to gather with others. For the Christian, it's crucial to make gathering with other Christians a high priority.

Rosaria Butterfield says, "Living in community is not just pleasant; it is life saving."[9] Indeed, Butterfield's salvation came through time spent with the people of God.[10]

Worship services are designed to build up of the body of Christ. Missionary and church planter's wife Gloria Furman says, "God ordains his Word to effectively do his bidding through preaching."[11] The New Testament instructs us to "devote [ourselves] to the public reading of Scripture, to exhortation, to teaching" (1 Tim. 4:13). God's means for growing his children is through the ordinary but powerful week-in-and-week-out gathering for the public proclamation of the Bible, worshiping him through song, enjoying communion together, joining in prayer, and sharing in other edifying activities.

It is to the church community that God gave pastors and teachers (and other leaders) "to equip the saints for the work of ministry, for building up the body of Christ . . . so that we may no longer be children, tossed to and fro by the waves and carried about by every wind of doctrine, by human cunning, by craftiness in deceitful schemes" (Eph. 4:12–14). Spiritual gifts—so called because they are imparted by the Holy Spirit who dwells in us—are meant to be exercised *in* the body and *for* the body. You and I have been equipped by

9. Rosaria Butterfield, *The Gospel Comes with a House Key: Practicing Radically Ordinary Hospitality in Our Post-Christian World* (Wheaton, IL: Crossway, 2018), 110.
10. See Rosaria Butterfield, *The Secret Thoughts of an Unlikely Convert: An English Professor's Journey Into Christian Faith* (Pittsburgh, PA: Crown & Covenant, 2012).
11. Gloria Furman, *The Pastor's Wife: Strengthened by Grace for a Life of Love* (Wheaton, IL: 2015), 90.

God to serve our brothers and sisters in Christ. And that can be done only as we gather together.

Gathering with the people of God allows our brothers and sisters in Christ to hold us accountable if we are caught in a transgression and restore us (Gal. 6:1–5). When we gather, we can encourage one another and build one another up (1 Thess. 5:11). In fact, there are fifty-nine commands in the New Testament for how Christians are to treat one another. Among other things, we are to greet one another with a holy kiss (Rom. 16:16), be kind and compassionate to one another (Eph. 4:2), and submit to one another out of reverence for Christ (Eph. 5:21). Jesus said, "By this all people will know that you are my disciples, if you have love for one another" (John 13:35).

Since my surrender to the Lord over twenty years ago, I have gathered nearly every week for church services, women's Bible study, small groups, and prayer times with a close friend or two. Much of the Spirit's work in our lives is through his people. Spiritual maturity is a community endeavor.

## Renewal Is Transformative

You and I are being shaped, either intentionally or covertly, by whatever we are consuming. As the adage goes, "We become what we behold."[12]

How can we obey the Bible's call to "set your minds on things that are above, not on things that are on earth" (Col. 3:2)? How can you and I toil with all the Spirit's energy

---

12. John M. Culkin, "A Schoolman's Guide to Marshall McLuhan," *Saturday Review*, March 18, 1967, 51–53, as quoted in John Stonestreet and Brett Kunkle, *A Practical Guide to Culture: Helping the Next Generation Navigate Today's World* (Colorado Springs: David Cook, 2017), chap. 14, Kindle edition.

in us, confessing our need for him in prayer, studying his word, and gathering with his people? As we commit to these practices, we will be changed from the inside out. We will be transformed by the renewing of our minds (Rom. 12:2).

Remember Shannon from chapter 3? She was my friend who met Christ while on a mission trip in Southeast Asia. Since that providential day over twelve years ago she has committed herself to these ordinary practices that bring about extraordinary change. The outward manifestation of the Spirit's transformation within includes Shannon starting a ministry for dancers in one of the most exploitive communities in our nation, becoming an internationally adoptive mom, teaching the Bible to others, regularly practicing hospitality and outreach in her secular neighborhood, and recently becoming a foster parent.

By the Spirit's power, Shannon was not only rooted in Christ, but she has toiled to renew her mind in Christ. She trusts God because she knows him, as the result of poring over his word. Her faith is strong because of God's grace through the people of God. She is truly transformed.

My obsession with the New Kids on the Block was silly and cringe-worthy. But that obsession shows how we are indeed transformed by what we love. My middle-school self conformed to the culture around me without any trouble at all. My context—the things I saw and heard and surrounded myself with—all preached a powerful NKOTB message, and I fell for it. Hard.

The good news is that a far better love can be crafted when we fix our hearts and minds on the right things. And the supreme thing is Jesus. With the Spirit's help, we can order our loves. When we are rooted in the gospel, and when we renew our minds in the gospel, we will be transformed by the gospel.

This rooting and renewing is how you and I build ourselves up in Christ. It's what will establish us in the faith and lead to the lasting joy we long for.

## Questions for Personal or Group Reflection

1. If you're discussing this book with a group, share your own cringe-worthy boy band obsession and enjoy a good laugh with one another.

2. What's your vision, conscious or perhaps subconscious, of the good life? Do you agree that we are what we love?

3. What cultural magnets woo you? In what way are your loves disordered?

4. Have your spiritual growth practices been primarily didactic, that is, intellectual and knowledge-based? What can

you do to pursue *loving* Jesus more with your heart? For example, for me, it's rising early to a quiet home, a cup of coffee, my Bible, and a journal to write my prayers.

5. Have you struggled with being like the Galatians: "Having begun by the Spirit, are you now being perfected by the flesh?" (Gal. 3:3). In other words, do you think grace is only for salvation, but not for sanctification?

6. Respond to the practices of confession and prayer, studying the word of God, and spending time with the people of God. Which ones do you do, want to do more, or resist? How can you and the sisters around you encourage one another to do those things more often? Pick some times and dates and practices right now, if you can.

7. Read Colossians 3:1–3 and Romans 12:1–2 and pray those things for yourself and others.

# 6

# Established in Christ

I'm learning to shop at the grocery store again. My family has been back in the United States for almost three years, but until just a few months ago, I couldn't set foot in a typical American grocery without feeling overwhelmed. For our first two years back I shopped only at Costco. Though the warehouse store is enormous, it offers a fraction of the food and options that a regular grocery does. The choices at our local grocery store stupefied me.

Take salad dressing for example. I took my kids to the salad dressing aisle and had them count the options while I shopped, just so I could make this point. They counted 199. There's creamy and oily, nonfat and full fat, organic, with red dye and without red dye, low sodium, name brand, and generic. The variations go on and on.

And salad dressing isn't the only culprit. Do you know how many cereal options there are? 261. Bread? 107.

My neighborhood market in Japan had an average of one choice per food item. If there were two choices, I went with the one that had a picture on the label, because I couldn't read the Japanese characters. Simple. Can you tell what's inside the package? Yes? Buy it. No? Move on and change your menu plan accordingly.

In America, and the West, choice is king.

## Choice: A God of Our Day

English author and social critic Os Guinness says, "Choice in modern life is central, powerful, unquestioned, and enshrined in how we think and all we do."[1] We know this is true because you and I have innumerable choices every day and everywhere we go. It's not just at the grocery store. Our choices are almost without limit at restaurants, when painting our fingernails, when enrolling our kids in sports, at the movies, at Starbucks, on television, and at the doctor. Whether we're considering food or churches or sports or schools—choice is king.

For us privileged people in the West, "life has become a smorgasbord with an endless array of dishes. And more important still, choice is no longer just a state of mind. Choice has become a value, a priority, a right. To be modern is to be addicted to choice and change. These are the unquestioned essence of modern life."[2] In our current cultural context, to be refused a choice is to be violated.

Don't get me wrong: options are good. I am grateful that I can choose how and where to educate my girls in the United States. I am relieved that we have choices for treating my daughter's scoliosis. It's important to me to vote and to voice my opinion in local politics. I have lived

---

1. Os Guinness, *The Call: Finding and Fulfilling the Central Purpose of Your Life* (Nashville: W Publishing Group, 1998), 167.
2. Guinness, *The Call*, 165.

in places where these options were not the norm, and it felt suffocating.

We in the West are convinced that choice will give us freedom, greater power, and even control. And in many ways it does. The market reveals the best option. The competition drives quality. The voices of the people make a real difference.

But have you noticed that rather than us owning our choices, they often own us? Rather than becoming truly free, we become trapped? We experience a sort of paralysis by analysis as we ponder all of the options available to us. And we feel immense pressure to make the very best choice, or else.

We not only ask, *What kind of cereal should I buy* but also, *What should I do with my life? Who am I? Which persona should I brand online? How can I determine and dictate my best life? How can I protect myself and those I love from all harm? How can I get the best for myself and my family?*

Choice itself isn't the problem. The problem arises when you and I begin to believe that we are omnipotent with our choice-making power. Like a mirage in the desert, choice casts an image of power that isn't backed up by our reality.

At first, the buffet of options looks attractive, but it ultimately makes us frenzied and frantic and fragile.

Because you and I are not God.

We are stymied by our lack of real power—clamoring over choices in hopes that we can rule our lives, but knowing deep down that we cannot. We don't have the actual power that we think choices give us. And so we're very tired. The modern person is exhausted from attempting to fill the vacuum of power with a substance that we simply don't have.

## Choice: The God Who Exhausts Us

The grocery store example of salad dressings is silly and lighthearted. But it represents the overwhelming array of options we have in our consumer-based culture. James K. A. Smith says we need to audit ourselves when it comes to choice. We need to assess the ethos of our households. What's the environment like in our homes? He says many households have "frantic rhythms . . . humming along with the consumerist myth of production and consumption."[3] We tend to believe that our worth is equal to what we can produce and consume. We look to ourselves, to the products we choose and buy, to the methods we choose to live by, to the things we can produce, and to the lifestyle choices we make for our value and identity.

As modern people we try to find our identity in what we can produce and consume, and we also look to our options and choices as the antidote to our fears. Afraid of something? There's an app for that. There's always *something* you can consume or produce to make your situation better. You have options.

We live by an equation of sorts: we fear something, we survey the options for fixing what we fear, we choose one, and we will it to work for our good.

For example, in our personal lives, we fear rejection from friends and family. So we try to be who they want us to be. We paint a persona that we believe they will love best.

3. James K. A. Smith, *You Are What You Love: The Spiritual Power of Habit* (Grand Rapids, MI: Brazos Press, 2016), 127.

You and I believe we can control the amount of acceptance, affection, and affirmation we get from them.

In our professional lives, we fear that we're not good enough, that our colleagues will find us out for the failures that we really are. So we clamor to prove ourselves, to make our names known. Ultimately, you and I believe we can control how others perceive us.

In our public lives, we fear not being liked—or should I say not getting enough likes? We want our name, our brand, our image to be admired. We filter photos, create captions, and crop real life, just so. My friend Carrie calls this "impression management." Again, you and I try to control what others think of us.

We fear a crash in the economy or job loss, and so we diversify investments, watch the stock market, scrimp and save and overspend. We fear global warming or deforestation or our own carbon footprint, and so we shop local, use cloth diapers, and ban plastic from our homes.

We fear a decline or crisis in our own personal health— cancer, depression, Alzheimer's, gaining too much weight, or whatever WebMD has diagnosed us with in the middle of the night. So we eat low carb, low fat, high fat, superfoods, no sugar, only sugar substitutes, no sugar substitutes. It's dizzying.

We fear what might happen to our children. We want only the very best for them. So we helicopter over our toddlers, ensure that every player gets a ribbon, coerce our kids' teachers when they get bad grades, and let them move back in when they fail to launch as young adults.

We worry about our own futures. We have IRAs and 401ks and long-term health insurance. We prepay for our funerals, write wills, and try to leave enough for our kids.

We have FOMO—fear of missing out on something fun right this very minute. So we stay tuned in to social media, text our friends, and document each moment.

Our fears range from the silly and superficial to life-or-death, eternity-in-the-balance kind of stuff. And our options for combating those fears come in many shapes and sizes. Our consumer culture markets myriad trouble-shooters to you and me. Everything from salad dressing to LinkedIn to just the right vitamin cocktail helps us to feel in control.

But at the end of the day, when we've studied all our choices, purchased the best we can find, and worked hard to prevent our deepest fears, we're left a bit hollow. When our heads hit the pillows, we suspect that we really don't have the ultimate say—that we can't actually produce or consume our way out of our deepest fears.

Doing all we can might not be enough. It's a heavy weight to bear.

## Chosen over Choosing

In response to our addiction to choice and the frenzy and fragility that comes with it, Os Guinness says, "Ultimately only one thing can conquer choice—being chosen."[4]

Only one thing can give us true peace: being chosen, rather than doing all the choosing ourselves.

Being chosen by whom? By God, the good and sovereign King of the universe. At the end of the day, it's God's choices that lead to real, lasting peace. This is especially true for the Christian. When we place all of our faith and hope in the Lord, he gives us a peace to guard our hearts that the world

---

4. Guinness, *The Call*, 167.

cannot understand (Phil. 4:7). We know that he is working all things for our good (Rom. 8:28). But even non-Christians experience the reality that God is active in our world. They may not have eyes to see, but he delivers common grace to all his creatures.

It's God's choices—his actions, his story, his will—that give peace, not our choices. God's good character, sovereignty, and will offer the only sufficient antidote to all of our fears. Following Christ "neutralizes the fundamental poison of choice in the modern life. 'I have chosen you,' Jesus said, 'you have not chosen me.' We are not our own, we have been bought with a price."[5] And so we who believe seek to follow Christ, not ourselves.

We are chosen. We don't have to put all our trust in our own choosing.

We know James, the brother of Jesus, was right when he said, "You do not know what tomorrow will bring. What is your life? For you are a mist that appears for a little time and then vanishes. Instead you ought to say, 'If the Lord wills, we will live and do this or that'" (James 4:14–15).

Indeed, we don't know what tomorrow will bring. We don't know if we'll be truly accepted by our loved ones. If we'll be considered good enough on the job. If our social media followers will "like" us. If the economy and environment and government will be strong and stable. If we'll be healthy and safe. If our kids will be okay. If our futures will be fine. If we're missing out on a life and a moment that's better than the one we're living.

But James says, *if the Lord wills*. We don't know about our lives and our futures. But God does. You and I can rest

5. Guinness, *The Call*, 167.

because God's will is good. What is his will? His will is good news. His will is the gospel. You and I can rest because of the gospel. We can rest because we are rooted, built up, and established in Christ.

## We Are Created, Called, and Accepted

Paul told the Romans, "There is therefore now no condemnation for those who are in Christ Jesus. For the law of the Spirit of life has set you free in Christ Jesus from the law of sin and death" (Rom. 8:1–2). We who have a relationship with Jesus and who have submitted to him are not condemned. We are free! There is no need for us to create a persona and identity that our friends and family might more readily accept. We've already been accepted by the most important person in the world—our Savior, our Creator, the one true God. Because of Jesus, our Father in heaven accepts us just as we are. You and I are already dearly and unconditionally loved.

As we saw in chapter 1, our current culture of self is a Siren call. The messaging all around us is that we should be self-made men and women who invent our true selves, our best selves. But this self-realization requires self-reliance, which is never quite enough. The good news is that you and I were created, and we're already called. We don't have to clamor to make up our identity—professional, public, or otherwise.

Ephesians 2 weaves together this truth with the good news of our acceptance. Paul tells the early church, "For by grace you have been saved through faith. And this is not your own doing; it is the gift of God, not a result of works, so that no one may boast. For we are his workmanship, created in Christ Jesus for good works, which God prepared beforehand, that we should walk in them" (Eph. 2:8–10).

We are created in Christ Jesus. We are saved by grace through faith. We are his workmanship, and he has already prepared good works for us to do. These few verses tell us how we got here, why we're here, and what we should be doing.

You and I don't have to wonder who we should be or what this life is all about. We don't have to clamor for purpose or meaning. John Calvin said, "We see that those who order their lives according to their own counsel have a restless disposition."[6] We can each picture restless times in our lives, can't we? We've been there. We know what it's like to try and answer life's big questions without God's wise and perfect counsel.

Self-invention and self-reliance are not necessary. In fact, they are contrary to what God has already given us. Our purpose and meaning and work were prepared in advance for us. Let's not say to the King, *no thank you*, but let's receive these good gifts and walk in them, experiencing great peace.

## Our God Is in Control Today

We can say with the psalmist, "Our God is in the heavens; / he does all that he pleases" (Ps. 115:3). When the Lord stretches out his hand, no one can turn it back. His will cannot be thwarted (Isa. 14:27).

Knowing that God is all-powerful as well as all good is what makes me able to sleep at night. When I worry about my daughters' well-being, whether or not my husband and

---

6. John Calvin, *A Little Book on the Christian Life*, trans. Aaron Denlinger and Burke Parsons (Sanford, FL: Reformation Trust, 2017), 46.

I made the right decisions, if we're going to be okay over-seas or back in America or wherever, if my loved ones who don't know Christ will meet him one day, I remember that God is able.

His power is equal to his goodness. And what better dis-play of that than the cross of Christ? The hands that hold our very lives are the same hands that were nailed to the cross. We have a Father who willingly gave up his Son for us. We serve a God who left heaven and laid down his own life for us. We can trust him. He is all powerful. And he is *all* good. He is the one and only good and powerful Creator and sustainer of all that is.

My father passed away right as I began writing this book. As far as I can tell, he died without ever trusting and believ-ing in God. Our gospel conversations never bore fruit that I could see. My dad's death outside of Christ was something I worried about daily through prayers, many tears, and pleas documented in my journals, for the three decades that I followed Jesus and my dad did not. I wondered if I would be able to trust the Lord and feel affection for him even if my dad died outside the faith.

When it finally came to pass, I found myself in the words of the Old Testament prophet Habakkuk: "Though the fig tree should not blossom, / nor fruit be on the vines, / the produce of the olive fail / and the fields yield no food, / the flock be cut off from the fold / and there be no herd in the stalls, / yet I will rejoice in the Lord; / I will take joy in the God of my salvation" (Hab. 3:17–18).

The words "the God of my salvation" remind me of who our God is. He is the God who saves. He is the God who left his throne in heaven on a rescue mission for you and me. He is the God who is willing to enter this messy space and bear my messy mistakes and love me unconditionally.

And so, with Habakkuk I can say, *even if*. Even if the worst comes to pass, even if the unthinkable happens, I will rejoice in the God of my salvation. The hands that bear nail wounds hold my life and yours. We can rest in that.

## Our God Is in Control Tomorrow

Proverbs 31 gives us a beautiful word picture of a woman who fears the Lord: "Strength and dignity are her clothing, and she laughs at the time to come" (Prov. 31:25). This woman is not worried about tomorrow, because she fears—or you could say respects or trusts—the Lord. She knows that his will is good, so she can look at the future with a smile. I want to be like her. I want to smile, to laugh, to be sure deep down in the depths of my soul that our God and his will are so good that tomorrow is laughable.

Jesus used another word picture to describe faith in God for the future. He said those who hear his words and do them will "be like a wise man who built his house on the rock. And the rain fell, and the floods came, and the winds blew and beat on that house, but it did not fall, because it had been founded on the rock" (Matt. 7:24–25). You probably already know that the fool who built his house on the sand lost it when the rains fell and the floods came and the winds blew.

To trust in God, to hear Jesus and obey him, is to build our futures on a sure foundation. This is what it means to be established in Christ. No matter what comes, we will stand, because he is a sure foundation.

### *We Have Every Spiritual Blessing*

We who are rooted in Christ also have every spiritual blessing in him in the heavenly places (Eph. 1:3). We need not
fear because we already have every blessing. Paul says in
his letter to the Ephesians that before the world was even
formed, God the Father chose us, adopted us as his children,
and lavished every spiritual blessing on us (Eph. 1:3–5).

First, what a relief that we were chosen before we
were even born—before the earth was even formed. You
and I did exactly nothing to receive our salvation in
Christ. God did it all. Second, not only are we adopted,
but we also have every spiritual blessing in him. Our
Father owns every spiritually good thing, and he's given
them all to us.

These spiritual blessings come to us through the Holy
Spirit, who lives in us (1 Cor. 3:16). On the night before
Jesus was crucified, he told his disciples, "The Helper, the
Holy Spirit, whom the Father will send in my name, he will
teach you all things and bring to your remembrance all that
I have said to you" (John 14:26).

Not only is the Holy Spirit our Helper and teacher, he's
also our peace giver. Jesus said, "Peace I leave with you; my
peace I give to you. Not as the world gives do I give to you.
Let not your hearts be troubled, neither let them be afraid"
(John 14:27). Jesus knew that trying times were ahead for
his disciples: persecution, rejection, martyrdom. But he did
not leave them—or us—without help and hope.

Spiritual blessings in heavenly places point us toward
our real home: heaven itself. Our natural bodies will one
day be raised spiritual bodies (1 Cor. 15:44). We will be imperishable (15:52) and have ultimate victory through Christ

Jesus (15:57). We will enjoy the gifts of heaven for eternity. We will live in a holy city with our God and "he will wipe away every tear from [our] eyes, and death shall be no more" (Rev. 21:4).

Between now and heaven we have the Holy Spirit in us who gives us power (Acts 1:8), helps us (John 15:26), prays for us (Rom. 8:26), gives us spiritual gifts for serving the church (1 Cor. 12:4–11), provides us with peace (John 14:27), produces spiritual fruit in our lives such as "love, joy, peace, patience, kindness, goodness, faithfulness, gentleness, [and] self-control" (Gal. 5:22–23), and more. Indeed, we have the Helper that Jesus promised.

## We Are People of Hope

Christian, we are different. We don't have to live like those who wonder if everything will be okay. We don't need to tie ourselves up in knots with worry about tomorrow. You don't have to worry about the unconditional acceptance of your family, the promotions at work, your baby's health, what college to go to, what city to live in, what life insurance policy to buy. While you and I will indeed still make those choices as active participants in our lives, our decisions don't dictate our futures. We can rest because our choices don't actually have the final say in any sphere—God has the final say. Remember, all things are through him and for him (Col. 1:16). *All* things.

We are people of hope. We have one—and only one—hope. But it's a huge hope, and it changes everything. It's the truth that Jesus Christ rose from the dead, and we will too. We are people of the resurrection. Rooted, built up, and established in Christ—this is our identity.

Peter, a disciple and intimate friend of Jesus, denied Jesus on the night he was betrayed, witnessed the resurrection, preached Jesus at Pentecost, became a leader of the early church, was imprisoned for Christ, and was ultimately martyred for his faith. During great persecution, Peter wrote, "According to [God's] great mercy, he has caused us to be born again to a living hope through the resurrection of Jesus Christ from the dead, to an inheritance that is imperishable, undefiled, and unfading, kept in heaven for you" (1 Pet. 1:3–4).

Peter rehearses the truth of his one and only hope in Jesus—the same hope he wanted the Christians who were dispersed by persecution to remember. He wanted those scattered for their faith to remember that they were people of hope. They were the people of the resurrection of Jesus. They were born again into his kingdom, and their inheritance was waiting—imperishable, undefiled, and unfading. They had every spiritual blessing then and in heaven.

Christians in the context of early Rome faced great threats, verbal abuse, physical mistreatment, and even death. So Peter told them to prepare their minds for action: "Set your hope fully on the grace that will be brought to you at the revelation of Jesus Christ" (1 Pet. 1:13). In other words, Jesus conquered death and he's coming back, and then we will receive our inheritance. Peter said to press on, friends! Put your hope in King Jesus. Commit your ways to him. Stay the course. We are a people of true, unfading hope.

## Pride Is the Enemy of Hope

At the closing of the same letter Peter told his readers, "Humble yourselves . . . casting all your anxieties on him, because he cares for you" (1 Pet. 5:6–7). To receive the care of Christ, you and I must be humble.

It has been said that "pride is the enemy of hope."[7] In our pride, we rely on ourselves. But we know our own limitations. Our own weaknesses. Our fragility. So does Jesus. And he cares for us. He cares so much, he willingly died in our place and receives us and our messes and our anxieties exactly as we are. We do not hope in ourselves. We do not place our hope in our ability to perfectly navigate our lives and our futures.

We put all our hope in our risen God.

## Applying Hope to Your Trial Today

As I write this, dear friends of mine are sitting in the pediatric intensive care unit with their thirteen-year-old son. They've been there with him for two weeks. Just about seventy-two hours before their world turned upside down, my husband and I were on a boat with them in Newport Harbor watching the sunset. We were with a handful of other pastors and their wives soaking up sweet fellowship, laughing, sharing stories and snacks, and living out one of those evenings that you never want to end (a foretaste of our promised inheritance, really).

After returning to Denver I got the news: a tumor had been found, and the son underwent surgery for aggressive cancer. Two weeks later he's still in the hospital. We get frequent alerts to pray for swelling, for bleeding, for infection, for nausea, for his life.

My husband and I are moved to tears and to pray. We went to seminary with these friends. We entered the

---

7. Andrew Delbanco, *The Real American Dream: A Meditation on Hope* (Cambridge, MA: Harvard University Press, 2000), 25, as quoted in Timothy Keller, *The Reason for God: Belief in an Age of Skepticism* (New York, Penguin, 2008), 161.

ministry when they did. Our kids are the same age, and two of them even share the same name. (Zoe, of course, because the dads were both in Greek class when those babies arrived!) When I see their family, I see mine. Same age. Same calling. Same kids. But where I have the luxury of currently healthy children, they're fighting for their young son's life.

But because they are people of hope, people of the resurrection, they fight from rest. With Paul they say, "But we have this treasure in jars of clay, to show that the surpassing power belongs to God and not to us. We are afflicted in every way, but not crushed; perplexed, but not driven to despair; persecuted, but not forsaken; struck down, but not destroyed; always carrying in the body the death of Jesus, so that the life of Jesus may also be manifested in our bodies" (2 Cor. 4:7–10).

Our friends see themselves accurately—as jars of clay. They are mere vessels that, in and of themselves, are not strong. But they carry the strongest power: God himself. They are afflicted, perplexed, persecuted, and struck down. But they are not crushed, despairing, forsaken, or destroyed. They have hope because they carry with them the death of Jesus, and also the life of Jesus. His life is everlasting and is imparted to you and me as well.

As my friends stand watch over their son twenty-four hours a day, as they make decisions with doctors and nurses at every turn, as they plead in prayer from their knees, as they do all that they humanly can for their son, they do so from rest. With Paul they remember that "the things that are seen are transient, but the things that are unseen are eternal" (2 Cor. 4:18). They are "of good courage" and "walk by faith, not by sight" (2 Cor. 5:6–7).

It's not that our friends believe their son will definitely be healed on earth. It's not that they put their hope in statistics or in the state-of-the-art medical care that's available to them. It's not that they don't care as much as other parents who might be found devastated by such news.

It's that their hope is in something certain—the most certain thing in the world: the life, death, and resurrection of Jesus. As resurrection people they rightly view their son's cancer as a "light momentary affliction [that] is preparing for [them] an eternal weight of glory beyond all comparison" (2 Cor. 4:17).

## Sleeping through the Storm

You may be facing a choice about what college major to pick, whether you should stay in a relationship or take a certain job, whether to enroll your child in a particular school, go to the mission field, jump into local politics, move your elderly parent into your home, serve in women's ministry, embrace a total or partial mastectomy—our choices are many. But at the end of the day we can rest—*really rest*—because we are established in Christ. He is in control. And he is good. And he is alive. He always ensures that his will comes to pass for our good and his glory.

Our friend, the father of the boy with cancer and a pastor himself, wrote these words:

> While the world offers many options of things to run to in these times, nothing the world offers works. Not really. Not ultimately. Nothing the world offers can bring the comfort, peace, healing, hope, and even joy we

so desperately (and I mean desperately) need in these darkest and scariest moments and seasons of life.

So, where must we run? For real?

We must run to our Maker. To our Creator. To our Savior. To the Lord our God. . . . Father, Son, and Holy Spirit.

He is the One. He is it.

Nothing and no one else will do.[8]

My friends are experiencing the peace Jesus promised to give. They are resting in his finished work. They have walked so many miles with their Savior that they are like him: sleeping through a storm (Matt. 8:23–27). They can truly rest because they know their good and powerful God, and they trust him.

Only one thing can cure the anxiety and fragility we experience as we try to control our own lives. That one thing is Jesus and him crucified, risen, and coming again. The antidote for the angst and dread and uncertainty of our day is knowing that he is the ultimate choice-maker in all things, he is good and powerful and kind, and that he loves us so much he laid down his life for us.

As we are established in him, so we can rest in him.

## Questions for Personal or Group Reflection

1. Where have you experienced the dizzying array of choices as I did in the American grocery store? Share laughable and serious examples.

---

8. Mark Hallock, November 26, 2018, https://www.facebook.com/mark ehallock/posts/2322280167800150.

2. Do you agree that choice has become a value, a priority, a right? Where do you see examples of people being addicted to choice?

3. What is good about choice? What can be bad about choice?

4. In what ways do you personally live by this equation: I fear something; I survey the options for avoiding what I fear; I choose an option; and I will it to work for my good?

5. Reflect on the following verses. Which ones give you the most peace and rest? Why?

Psalm 115:3

Proverbs 31:25

Habakkuk 3:17–18

136 Established in Christ

Matthew 7:24–27


John 14:26–27


Romans 8:1–2


Ephesians 2:8–10


Ephesians 1:3–6


6. How is pride the enemy of hope?



7. We Christians are a people of hope. Read 2 Corinthians 4:7–10 and reflect on how God is giving you hope in a specific trial.

8. How can you better practice setting your mind on the "inheritance that is imperishable, undefiled, and unfading, kept in heaven for you" (1 Pet. 1:4)?

# Finding Lasting Joy

When my husband and I were dating, he saved up his money and purchased a used car that he had wanted for a long time. We're talking late 1990s, so it was the very popular, very dark purple Volkswagen Jetta. He had had his eye on it for as long as I had known him. It would be his mature, adult car—a significant move up from the Geo Storm he had been driving.

After years of scrimping and scraping, he finally brought home his pride and joy and parked it in front of the house he was renting. When I arrived on the scene, I eagerly asked if I could take it for a spin. With just a hint of hesitation, Mark said okay. It was stick shift and so fun. German engineering.

I returned the very popular, very dark purple Volkswagen Jetta to the front of his house and put the sparkly new treasure in reverse to avoid blocking the driveway.

*Crunch.*

I had not noticed the other car. I smooshed the new-to-him back bumper, and chipped the (what turned out to be very expensive) very popular, very dark purple paint. I still feel anxiety thinking about it twenty years later.

What had been a source of great joy one minute became a great disappointment the next.

## Disneyland: The Happiest Place on Earth

Perhaps the best place to observe fleeting moments of happiness is Disneyland. It's where you can watch a toddler go from wild-eyed excitement to wild-eyed anger in less than five seconds. One second the little guy is hugging Goofy, and the next second he's kicking and screaming because his ice cream cone fell to the ground. Joy to sorrow in record time.

It's not just the toddlers. It's the big kids too. They go from screams of exultation on Space Mountain to screaming *shut up* to their siblings in the next long line. Parents aren't exempt either. I have actually heard myself say, "Oh, yes you are going on that ride, little missy. Mommy didn't spend all this money so you could chicken out now!" I know. Proud moment.

Disneyland is sparkly clean. All of the staff, or "cast members" as they are called, are all smiles all the time. The sights, smells, and sounds keep your mind moving from one joy to the next. The parades and Mickey-shaped pretzels and beautiful landscaping make a solid attempt at perfection. It might actually be *the* happiest place on earth.

And yet, no one gets away from Disneyland without a temper tantrum or meltdown. Moms and dads, grandmas and grandpas, big sisters, little brothers. None of us can make it through a day at Disney, or anywhere for that matter, unscathed.

## Earthly Joy Fades

We live for moments of joy—both the profound and the simple. You and I and every other human on the planet search daily for the things that will make us happy. Advertisers and girlfriends and social media tell us where to find them. So many ideas and life hacks and products promise to be life changing, joy giving.

I'd venture to say that we spend most of our waking hours looking for ways to be happy, the secret to our satisfaction, and how to be fulfilled. *If I can just get the kids down and have a cup of coffee, I'll be happy. If I can just get this paper turned in, I'll be happy. If I can just make it to Friday night, I'll be happy. If I can just get into that school . . . get hired for that job . . . marry that guy . . . buy a house in that neighborhood . . . save enough money to buy that purse.*

What's tricky about these moments of joy, though, is that they're temporary. That naptime, that life hack, that diploma, that raise last only so long. Sooner or later, and often way before we're ready, their luster fades.

We all have very popular, very dark purple Jettas, don't we? The doll's hair gets tangled. The dinosaur's leg breaks off. The backpack that all the cool kids are wearing gets stained by a Sharpie. The superexpensive, famous-athlete-endorsed tennis shoes are in fashion for only one month before the next model comes out. The must-have baby product for perfect parents gets recalled. The new iPhone screen cracks.

But it's not just stuff. Even people and traditions and lifestyles disappoint. Your dear friend starts to avoid you. Your sister's values grow to be the exact opposite of your own. Your husband stays late at the office—again. Your children talk back. Your mentor falls. Your pastor gives in to temptation. The Christmas turkey burns. The birthday gift is not at all what you asked for. Your church has changed. Your neighbors have turned on you. Your job feels like a waste of time. The earthquake. The forest fire. The recession. The job loss. The illness. The sudden death.

Where in the world can you and I find *lasting* joy?

## Our Small, Safe Faith Cycle

All Christians must come to that moment, discussed in chapter 3, when we realize that the joy we seek in the world is fleeting. This moment leads to us being rooted in Christ, built up in him, and established in him. It's in this moment that the happiness provided through things or people or accomplishments runs out and, in his mercy, Jesus calls us to himself. It's God's kindness to reveal our need for him.

We hit bottom, and we know that God will help us, so we turn to him. We take a deep breath and whisper a prayer for patience at work. Or we pause in the pantry and ask the Spirit to intervene in our anger.

We become aware that *somehow* joy is found only in Jesus.

But what if we turn to a god who is made of a substance that we invent and impose on him, unaware? A god with attributes that we accidentally conjure up? A savior who unintentionally, but remarkably, resembles a slightly better version of *us*?

Here's what I often see in myself and in others: we turn to a god made in our image—a god who is safe and small and primarily interested in our comfort, security, and success. A god who wants to bless our best efforts. A god who wants us to be healthy and arrive safely at every destination and achieve every milestone in the American dream.

This god would never ask us to do anything crazy. This god wouldn't ask us to endure hardship. This god is only for our good—and we define what that "good" looks like.

I'm not sure which comes first here, the god we invented, the faith we have in him, or the calling we think he's given us, but they all feed each other in an ongoing cycle. The god in our image is safe and small. The faith we have in him is weak and meager. The callings we pursue are doable with our own strength and power. In this way, we keep our faith journey manageable, under our own control. It's a pursuit of joy with little risk.

I am as attracted to this small cycle as anyone. The goals in my community are health, good education for our kids, a strong retirement account, and plenty of sports on the weekends. We're all cheering for one another as we chase our small dreams and claim that it's what our small god would want.

Here's the telltale sign that our god, our faith, and our calling are small and self-created: we find ourselves at the center of them all. You and I must ask ourselves if the values of our god are identical to our own. Have we reworded the Bible so that it matches our preferences, rather than us being changed by it? Are we living exactly like our non-Christian friends and family and simply slapping a #blessed on all we do? Are we being stretched beyond ourselves?

In our quest for joy, are we living for our own glory, our own name, our own success? Can we honestly say that our Christianity requires *faith*? Because what Jesus asks of us requires great faith. He asks you and me to die. And in that death, he promises joy.

We concluded in chapter 1 that the Siren call of self is a strong one. In Greek mythology the Sirens were magnets to sailors, causing them to be shipwrecked on the rocky cliffs. Today, my self-preservation, self-exaltation, and self-promotion are Siren calls that are hard to resist. When I draw too close to them, my joy is shipwrecked.

Self is the Siren that keeps nonbelievers—and even believers—from lasting joy.

## Jesus Wrecks the Small Cycle

Jesus destroys our small, safe faith cycle when he says, "If anyone would come after me, let him deny himself and take up his cross and follow me. For whoever would save his life will lose it, but whoever loses his life for my sake and the gospel's will save it" (Mark 8:34–35). This calling to

deny ourselves, to take up our crosses, and to follow Jesus
is neither small nor manageable.

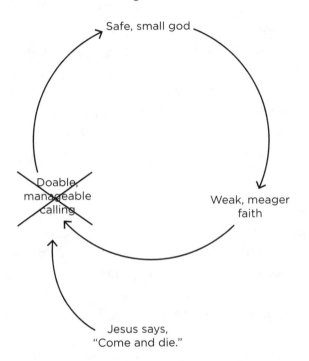

The truth is that Scripture calls us to live out a big, risk-
taking, self-denying cycle. To answer this call we need a huge
God who is capable of doing huge things in us and through
us. We need a faith that is robust and doesn't reject hard
things—a faith that acknowledges that the hard things are,
in fact, what God has designed for our good and his glory.

And here's the kicker. Here's the life-changing paradox
of the Christian faith. This—*this!*—is where lasting joy is
found: When you and I are rooted in the gospel, built up
in the gospel, and established in the gospel—when you and
I believe in our big God, are sustained by great faith that

only he can give, and lay down our lives to respond to his big call—we find joy.

*Whoever loses his life for my sake will save it.*

But before we ponder the great paradox of genuine faith—namely, that dying to oneself leads to lasting joy— let's first remind ourselves of God's call on us to identify with our Savior. Let's remember that Jesus does, in fact, insist that his true followers bear their own crosses.

We need the reminder because, let's be honest, this truth is often lost in our comfortable, Western Christian context.

## Jesus Really Does Say Come and Die

Os Guinness says, "For many believers the Christian life is now the good life: It simply 'goes better with Jesus' even if there is no God and no Resurrection."[1] This is why we have to ask ourselves if our lives look any different than our non-Christian neighbors and friends and family. Are we living distinctly Christian lives? Do we really seek to take after Jesus?

The distinctly Christian life is one wholly surrendered to the Lord. Not perfectly, of course. We won't reach perfection until heaven. But is your life marked by an ever-increasing desire to look like our Savior?

German pastor and theologian Dietrich Bonhoeffer famously said in his book *The Cost of Discipleship*, "When Christ calls a man, he bids him come and die."[2] A vocal dissenter of the Nazis precisely because of his identity with Christ, Bonhoeffer was executed by hanging in a concentration camp just before the end of World War II.

---

1. Os Guinness, *The Call: Finding and Fulfilling the Central Purpose of Your Life* (Nashville: W Publishing Group, 1998), 209.
2. Dietrich Bonhoeffer, *The Cost of Discipleship* (New York: Touchstone, 1959), 89.

While Bonhoeffer and countless other Christians have died a martyrdom by blood, we're all called to *at least* a martyrdom characterized "by abandoning everything for the love of God. Discipleship therefore means a . . . funeral of our own independence."[3]

Jesus's bid to us is like that of his Father's to him. Jesus can be our Messiah because he came and died. Salvation comes through death. And we can be his disciples only if we do the same. We are saved by his death, and sanctified in a million smaller deaths of our own as we follow him.

We see this call to die time and time again in the Bible. We are called to put to death our independence and live under the lordship of Christ. You won't find this message featured on coffee mugs or on throw pillows or in best sellers, but it's in the pages of Scripture:

"Whoever loves his life loses it, and whoever hates his life in this world will keep it for eternal life." (John 12:25)

"Do you not know that all of us who have been baptized into Christ Jesus were baptized into his death?" (Rom. 6:3)

"I die every day!" (1 Cor. 15:31)

"I have been crucified with Christ. It is no longer I who live, but Christ who lives in me." (Gal. 2:20)

"For you have died, and your life is hidden with Christ in God." (Col. 3:3)

Choosing death is not natural for us. We want safety and comfort and success on the small cycle. I pop an Advil anytime I'm threatened by a headache. We wear seatbelts. We buy recliners. We put nets on our kids' trampolines

---

3. Guinness, *The Call*, 207.

and helmets on their heads. We seek protection, not death. But when it comes to our spiritual lives, Jesus commands the opposite.

If your devotional book, your women's Bible study, your pastor, your favorite Christian author, or your Christian best friend doesn't encourage you to come and die, an alarm should go off in your head. If their messages are for self-preservation and self-promotion, you know they don't match God's word. If they want to bless you on the small cycle, you know it's not the life Jesus has for you.

## How Sin Keeps Us Caught in the Small Cycle

Sin insists that my way is better than God's way. For many of us Christians, sin is a commitment to the small cycle and an unwillingness to be wrecked by Jesus's call.

Guinness puts it this way: "Sin is 'the claim to the right to myself'—and therefore . . . the root of a profound and inescapable relativism."[4] In other words, when we say, "My god would never command this" or, "My Jesus would never do that," or when we challenge, "Did God actually say that?," we sin. The small cycle of faith is as old as Adam and Eve.

Exodus 20:3 says, "You shall have no other gods before me." But when you and I insist on managing our faith and controlling the call and commands of our God, we put ourselves before him. We inwardly answer, *No, God didn't actually say that. He doesn't really want me to die.* And often, the Christian culture machine around us reinforces this view. Sin is seeking to invent myself rather than to resemble my Savior and Creator.

---

4. Guinness, *The Call*, 204.

If you and I are going to be willing to come and die as Jesus insists, then we must first be convinced that following him is better than following ourselves. His words matter more than our own. His will is higher than ours. We submit to him. To submit and surrender and suffer is to be radically countercultural. To pursue Jesus's name and glory, even unto suffering and death, is to be seen by the world (and even sometimes the church) as a fool for Christ (1 Cor. 4:10).

Dying to oneself is not only radically countercultural. It's also radically counterintuitive. Pursuing death and pain goes against our flesh, our intuition, and all that is naturally within us.

But Christ calls us, and the Spirit enables us, and the Father is pleased with us when we obey. It is there—in the cross-bearing—that you and I experience the great paradox of genuine faith.

In God's economy, dying to oneself leads to lasting joy.

## Gospel-Fueled Joy

In her book *The Pastor's Wife*, Gloria Furman says to women, "Only the mercy shown to us at the cross can inspire us to build our home under the headship of our husband to the glory of Christ."[5] While she's speaking specifically to wives and in the context of marriage, these words are strikingly applicable to all Christians for every act in the Christian life.

Only the mercy shown to us at the cross can inspire us to do *anything* that requires surrender or submission or suffering. Naturally, you and I would never move toward

---

5. Gloria Furman, *The Pastor's Wife: Strengthened by Grace for a Life of Love* (Wheaton, IL: Crossway, 2015), 87.

self-denial. But we can't help but be moved for Jesus's sake when we consider that it was "for our sake he made him to be sin who knew no sin, so that in him we might become the righteousness of God" (2 Cor. 5:21).

Our sin for his righteousness. Our darkness for his light. Our destruction for his restoration. Our deserved death for his everlasting life. Hell for heaven.

When we remember the gospel, we can't help but be grateful! We can't help but be joyful!

Indeed, this is the heart of Paul's message to the Colossians. He instructed them, "As you received Christ Jesus the Lord, so walk in him, rooted and built up in him and established in the faith, just as you were taught, abounding in thanksgiving" (Col. 2:6–7).

Those very words are the inspiration and structure of this book, and they're exactly where you and I can find lasting joy. We received Christ by overwhelming grace (Col. 2:6). While we were his enemies, he died for us. And we walk in overwhelming grace as God himself supplies all that we need. If we are rooted in this overwhelming, undeserved, amazing grace, built up in it, and have our lives established in it, we will abound in thanksgiving (Col. 2:7). This gratitude will necessarily lead to lasting joy.

This rooted, built-up, and established joy will never lose its luster.

We abound in thanksgiving when we meditate on the gospel, history's greatest exchange. As the old hymn says, "Jesus paid it all, all to him we owe; / sin had left a crimson stain, he washed it white as snow."[6] And joy comes. It comes flooding

---

6. Elvina M. Hall, "Jesus Paid It All," 1865.

in with the everlasting life and the indwelling Spirit and the pleasure of God when we remember that Jesus paid it all.

Knowing that "God, being rich in mercy, because of the great love with which he loved us, even when we were dead in our trespasses, made us alive together with Christ" (Eph. 2:4–5) makes us willing to do anything that Jesus asks of us. The gospel confirms for us his kindness and character and trustworthiness, so that we are ready and even eager to lay down our lives for him.

It's in the gospel that we recognize that our lives are fleeting. Our energy and power and self-help are small and temporal. But Jesus's story and life and power and purpose are eternal. He is forever and ever, amen. Lasting joy is found in him.

## The Big, Self-Denying Faith Cycle

It's remembering and rehearsing the gospel that makes us willing to get off the small, safe, self-invented, self-manageable cycle and trust in Jesus. It's remembering and rehearsing the gospel that makes us willing to lose our own lives to find real life.

Gospel-fueled joy reminds you and me that we serve a big God who gives us a big faith and enables us to answer his big call on our lives. Gospel-fueled joy prefers and prioritizes self-denial because it knows and believes that it's better to give than to receive (Acts 20:35).

The calling Jesus gives his followers—to deny ourselves and to lose our lives—will present itself in as many unique ways as there are unique Christians. Our God is creative, and we are his workmanship (Eph. 2:10). Our callings will be as diverse as we are—but they will all demand that we deny ourselves.

Your calling may be coping well with what God ordains in your life, such as serving your family or neighbors, walking through a terminal diagnosis, or stewarding well your abundance. Or your calling may take you out of the ordinary—to the mission field, to work among the impoverished, or to adoption.

As Christ-followers we don't know what tomorrow will hold. We can't be sure what Jesus will ask of us. But we can know that it will require you and me to deny ourselves, pick up our crosses, and die with him. In the 1500s John Calvin said, "Those whom the Lord has chosen and condescended to welcome into fellowship with him should prepare themselves for a life that is hard, laborious, troubled, and full of many and various kinds of evil."[7]

Indeed, the Christian life is hard. To trust in Jesus when your young son suffers from cancer is hard. To trust in

7. John Calvin, *A Little Book on the Christian Life*, trans. Aaron Denlinger and Burke Parsons (Sanford, FL: Reformation Trust, 2017), 57.

Jesus when your father dies outside of saving faith is hard. To move your family overseas to a dark place and shine the light of Christ is hard. To adopt traumatized children out of foster care is hard. To love your enemies is hard. To give sacrificially is hard. But when Christ-followers "cast themselves on the grace of God, they experience the presence and power in which there is sufficient and abundant help."[8]

When we run out of self-preservation, self-help, and self-pity, Jesus is there. He freely gives his presence and power. He is our help. He will never leave us or forsake us (Heb. 13:5).

## Peter: Jesus-Denier, Then Self-Denier

Peter was one of Jesus's closest friends and dearest disciples. He left his life to follow Christ full time (Matt. 4:18). He ventured out and walked on water to Jesus (Matt. 14:29). Clearly, he put all his hope in Jesus.

And yet, on the night that Jesus was taken into custody, Peter denied being associated with him—three times (Luke 22:54–62). Self-preservation won out, and in fear Peter distanced himself from his Lord.

But because of God's great mercy and providence, Jesus triumphed over death, was resurrected, and reappeared to Peter, the other disciples, and hundreds of others. In view of Jesus's great power and mercy, Peter committed himself anew to Christ and to the proclamation of the gospel.

Peter boldly preached the gospel in front of a multitude on the day of Pentecost (Acts 2:14–41) such that three thousand new believers were baptized. Peter's continued bold preaching landed him in prison, but even that couldn't

---

8. Calvin, *Little Book on the Christian Life*, 62.

stop him. He proclaimed, "We must obey God rather than men" (Acts 5:29), and he kept on doing just that. Ultimately, he found himself in Rome, under the reign of the vicious emperor Nero, and facing certain death.

Calvin says, "When [Peter] reflected on the savage death that he would suffer, he was struck with horror, and would have willingly run away. But the thought that he was called to that death by God's own command then came to his aid, conquering and trampling his fear, so that he willingly and cheerfully submitted himself to death."[9]

Peter, who was admittedly timid and self-interested at times, upon remembering the gospel, laid down his life with joy for Jesus's name. Church history and common tradition say that he requested to die by an upside-down crucifixion, feeling unworthy to die the same way that his Lord did. Peter was rooted, built up, and established in the faith, which led to gratitude and great joy and a willingness to give his life for his Lord.

You and I are not likely to face an upside-down crucifixion. But will we face whatever God asks of us with joy? Will we allow ourselves to be propelled by gospel gratitude away from self and toward our Lord? Will we unwrap our white knuckles from self-preservation and remember him who knew no sin and took on ours, and then happily give our lives to him?

## For the Joy Set before Us

It was for the *joy set before him* that Christ endured the cross (Heb. 12:2). Again: Jesus *willingly* endured the cross for you and me because of *joy*. He fixed his eyes on the joy that

---

9. Calvin, *Little Book on the Christian Life*, 81.

would come from laying down his life. The writer of Hebrews tells us to "consider him who endured from sinners such hostility against himself, so that you may not grow weary or fainthearted" (Heb. 12:3). When we consider Jesus—when we remember the gospel and are driven by the gratitude and joy that results—we will not grow fainthearted.

If our God turned his death into joy, then we can trust him to do the same with ours. For the joy set before us, we can carry our cross. Indeed, there's no other way to get lasting joy.

Joy comes from cross-carrying.

Chances are, for you and me, this pursuit of joy through death will entail dying a thousand small deaths every day. Honoring our parents when we're sure they're wrong. Respecting our professors who defame our God. Waking in the middle of the night for the baby. Greeting our husband with a kiss in the evening after he hurt our feelings in the morning. Serving our bosses who only serve themselves.

James K. A. Smith says, "Too often we look for the Spirit in the extraordinary when God has promised to be present in the ordinary."[10] The Spirit will fill us with joy as we abide in him, walk with him, and serve him rather than ourselves in myriad ways each day. It doesn't have to be complicated. It's giving a cup of cold water in his name. It's kindness.

It's loving God and loving neighbor more than self.

You and I who are in Christ are not captive to the fading joys of this world. We are not beholden to very dark purple Jettas and trips to Disneyland and afternoon coffee while the kids nap. By all means, enjoy the new car and the family

---

10. James K. A. Smith, *You Are What You Love: The Spiritual Power of Habit* (Grand Rapids, MI: Brazos Press, 2016), 67.

vacation and the delicious cup of coffee; I certainly do! But we must remember that while those things are good and worthy of our enjoyment, they are not ultimate.

Our ultimate joy does not come from here. Our lasting joy is not temporary. It is not self-made.

Jesus gave us this promise: "If you keep my commandments, you will abide in my love, just as I have kept my Father's commandments and abide in his love. These things I have spoken to you, *that my joy may be in you, and that your joy may be full*" (John 15:10–11). These words were spoken by the God-man who hung on a cross for you and me and for his own joy. We can trust his words. We can believe what Jesus says. If we lay down our lives and walk in his commands, his joy will be in us, our joy will be full.

Lasting joy exists. It is there for the finding and receiving. It comes from the hands of the giver of life. It is for you and for me and for all who resist the Siren call of self.

In this age of self, enough about you and me. May we be so rooted, so built-up, and so established in the gospel that our gratitude abounds and our joy is full.

## Questions for Personal or Group Reflection

1.  Where do you tend to look for fleeting joy? In a cup of coffee, a new car, your career? Talk about how those are not bad things. They are good gifts and meant to give us pleasure, but they are not the source of lasting joy.

2.  Do you find yourself on the small cycle? Do you find yourself trying to follow Christ but with little to no risk? Can you honestly say that you need faith for what you believe God has called you to?

3.  What do you think when you consider Jesus's words in Mark 8:34–35? How do you feel about losing your life, taking up your cross? Be open and honest and invite your sisters in Christ to help you wrestle through what causes you to pursue self-preservation or encourages you to embrace self-denial.

4.  How does the mercy shown to us at the cross inspire us to do anything that requires surrender or submission or suffering?

5.  Describe a time when God has enabled you to be on the big cycle. What was it like to see God as big, to have big faith, to answer a big call? Have you stayed on the big cycle? Has it expanded? Have you hopped off?

6.  Reflect on Peter's life. How does he encourage you?

7.  Do you really believe that if our God turned his death into joy, then we can trust him to do the same with ours? For the joy set before you, are you ready to carry your cross? Share with your friends what that cross is and ask them to pray with you for the faith to follow through.

8.  In the age of self, what's your plan for pursuing lasting joy? Pray and ask the Spirit to lead you and enable you in this lifelong and worthy pursuit.

# Conclusion

"Do what makes you happy."

Featured on Instagrammable photos, chalkboards, and journal covers, this used to seem like great advice. Except we tried it. And it didn't work.

We tried more me-time. More coffee breaks. More yoga. More fulfilling careers. Better pay. Better childcare. Nicer homes. Ergonomic baby carriers. Delayed marriage. Early marriage. No marriage. Maybe the paleo diet. Or the keto diet. Or maybe more carbs. More exercise. More naps.

We Western women have supped at the buffet of options. We really have tried to figure this thing out. As much as we "do what makes you happy," we're still falling short. It's not delivering. In fact, studies show that we're less happy than ever.

Now we know it's because we weren't actually made to live for ourselves. You and I were made in the image of God to live for his glory; we are characters in *his* story. As a several-hundred-year-old church confession says, we're here to glorify God and enjoy him forever.[1] Our good and God's glory are connected.

---

1. Westminster Shorter Catechism (Q. 1).

Our God—our author and Redeemer—is merciful and powerful and just and trustworthy, and he relentlessly pursued (and daily pursues) you and me. As we walk in his image—as we live out our life purpose—it will be for his glory and not our own. Our joy comes as we image Jesus.

Jesus, who left his throne in heaven and willingly lived the perfect life that you and I could never live, willingly hung on a cross to pay for your sins and mine, and rose victorious from the grave, says, "Whoever finds his life will lose it, and whoever loses his life for my sake will find it" (Matt. 10:39).

The good life is found in losing it. If you and I are going to be happy, our lives must be hidden in Christ Jesus (Col. 3:3). It is for our good to enjoy God and to bring him glory.

Maybe the popular saying should be tweaked to say, "Do what makes you *holy*."

Or how about, "Do what makes you holy, because that will ultimately make you happy, because Jesus, who is the giver of life, says that true life is found in carrying your cross, after him."

It's not very catchy. It isn't likely to sell many throw pillows at Target. But it's the truth. Self-denial, cross-carrying, is where you and I will find the lasting joy we long for.

## No One Drifts toward Holiness

But this cross-carrying—this living for God's glory—does not come naturally to you and to me. Though it is in fact for our good, no one drifts toward cross-carrying. Theologian and professor D. A. Carson says:

> People do not drift toward Holiness. Apart from grace-driven effort, people do not gravitate toward godliness,

prayer, obedience to Scripture, faith, and delight in the Lord. We drift toward compromise and call it tolerance; we drift toward disobedience and call it freedom; we drift toward superstition and call it faith. We cherish the indiscipline of lost self-control and call it relaxation; we slouch toward prayerlessness and delude ourselves into thinking we have escaped legalism; we slide toward godlessness and convince ourselves we have been liberated.[2]

Put another way, we drift toward self. Holiness requires intentionality. If we are going to pursue lasting joy, we must be rooted, built up, and established in the gospel. And this requires grace-driven effort, as Carson says. It requires the Holy Spirit's help, the submission of our flesh, the abandonment of ourselves as our highest priority.

Apart from Jesus we can do nothing (John 15:5). We must abide in him, and he in us. We must constantly renew our minds through the Word of God, the people of God, and with the help of the Spirit of God. In this way, we push against the riptide that pulls us into the small cycle. Through grace-driven effort—the spiritual disciplines empowered by the Holy Spirit—we can swim against the current of culture and flesh and establish ourselves on the big cycle.

## The Big Cycle Expands

The remarkable thing about the big cycle is that it expands. It does not stay the same, circular shape. It grows outward, like a hurricane. That's spiritual growth, or

---

2. D. A. Carson, *For the Love of God: A Daily Companion for Discovering the Riches of God's Word* (Wheaton, IL: Crossway Books, 1998), 2:23.

sanctification. As Paul says, "Our inner self is being re-newed day by day" (2 Cor. 4:16).

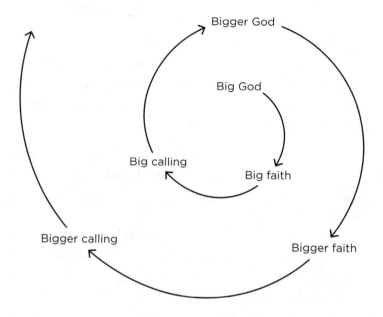

As you and I grow in our understanding of our big God, our faith gets bigger, and we are equipped to answer his big call. At that point, though, we don't go back to our original understanding of God. Our understanding expands. Our faith expands. And our calling expands. The more we know him, the more we trust him, and the more we are enabled and empowered and willing to do in his name.

We grow up in our salvation from infancy to maturity (1 Pet. 2:2). The taking off of the old self and the putting on of the new self is not a one-time event (Eph. 4:22–24). It is a lifelong pursuit that grows, our faith radiating farther and farther, God's glory becoming brighter and brighter, our joy going deeper and deeper.

Think of Peter. As a brand-new Christian he needed much faith to abandon his life and follow Jesus. But as he grew to know his Lord better and better, his faith also grew. He began to believe that Jesus really could heal the sick and feed the hungry. He then had faith to preach Christ boldly and to suffer imprisonment and the rejection of his countrymen. He ultimately had faith to be crucified upside down in Jesus's name.

The same is true for your faith journey and mine. We might struggle at first to pursue seemingly small tasks that Jesus entrusts to us. We might quake at the thought of bringing up God's name at the family reunion. But then we try it—and our understanding of God grows, our faith grows, and our calling grows. So we start telling our co-workers and neighbors and friends about Jesus too. One day we find ourselves sharing the gospel with our enemy, a prisoner, a nonbeliever in a dark country far away. Our big cycle expands.

I think of my friend Shannon. She joined a bunch of girlfriends on a mission trip to Southeast Asia and there she met Christ. Her Christian journey proved God faithful time and time again. Her track record with the Lord gave way to greater and greater callings. After her time in Southeast Asia she had faith to share the love of Jesus with exploited women, then to lead Bible studies, then to adopt a daughter from overseas, then to proclaim Christ at neighborhood events, then to bring home three older siblings for foster care. Shannon didn't go from zero to one hundred over night. The Lord wooed her to the big cycle. She believed he is who he says he is. She trusted him and stepped out. One leap of faith led to another. Shannon now bears witness to the Lord's faithfulness in countless acts and adventures that he's led her on. Her life is a light, a city on a hill (Matt. 5:13–16).

What is the next act of faith that God is calling you to? Where might you grow in your faith and believe that God is who he says he is? We are all called to great faith, but the acts of faith will vary. You may need to exercise great faith in your home, your office, your marriage, your neighborhood. Or you may be called to exercise great faith across town, across the globe, across several comfort zones. Our lives and our callings are unique and diverse. But we are all called.

The world tells us to look within for our joy, to rely on ourselves for our happiness, to bring about our own meaning and success. But that cycle gets smaller and smaller, turns in on itself, and ultimately snuffs out your life and mine. That's exactly what landed me on my dorm room floor. But God, in his mercy and power, lifted my eyes from myself to him. It was in beholding him, that joy came.

God is so gracious to grow us and change us as we walk with him. Lasting joy comes from that journey, and he's eager to provide it to you and to me. Life in Christ—*real* life, the losing of this life for the gaining of his—is the powerful antidote that stands ready to respond to the discouragement and disillusionment created by the age of self.

May we turn to our giver of life for lasting joy. May we embrace grace-driven disciplines that root us, build us up, and establish us in the faith. May our faith, and therefore our joy, grow and expand and radiate in the days and years to come.

# General Index

# Scripture Index